HOW TO CHEAT IN SPORTS

Professional Tricks Exposed!

by SCOTT OSTLER

Foreword by Rick Reilly • Illustrations by Arthur Mount

CHRONICLE BOOKS
SAN FRANCISCO

Text copyright © 2008 by Scott Ostler.
Foreword copyright © 2008 by Rick Reilly.
Illustrations copyright © 2008 by Arthur Mount.

Library of Congress Cataloging-in-Publication
Data available.

ISBN: 978-0-8118-5853-3

Manufactured in China.

Designed by River Jukes-Hudson

10 9 8 7 6 5 4 3 2 1

Chronicle Books LLC
680 Second Street
San Francisco, California 94107

www.chroniclebooks.com

Dedicated to my late dad, Don Ostler, the last honest man.

CH. 1 FOOTBALL 13

CH. 2 BASKETBALL 37

CH. 3 BASEBALL 77

CH. 4 MISCELLANEOUS 131

FOREWORD
Rick Reilly

I didn't write this foreword. Scott Ostler did. But I'm putting my name on it. That's the kind of cheating I learned from Scott.

Have you ever played basketball with this man? Aside from his questionable use of elbows, his knack for grasping your shirt and shorts for leverage, and his habit of flopping like a Barry Bonds musical, he's really very strict about the rules.

Yet here he is, writing a very funny how-to book on sports cheating. Imagine that—celebrating cheating at a time when the purity of sport is under question. But maybe it's not as simple as that. Perhaps he believes by shining a light on the dark world of cheating, a more informed sports fan can watch for it, and tipped-off athletes can counter it. Then again, we *are* talking about Scott, so he's probably just doing it to pay off his bookies.

It figures that one of the best sportswriters in San Francisco history would write a book about cheating, in that San Francisco is to cheating what Sheboygan is to bratwurst. Gaylord Perry of the Giants used to throw a spitter that needed triple-ply Bounty by the time it got to the plate. Barry Bonds' records in the book should all have tiny syringes next to them. Victor Conte and his Bay Area BALCO lab will go down as the Henry Ford of Fraud.

I do understand why people cheat in sports. Whether you're playing in the Super Bowl or a weekend touch-football mud bowl, competitive juices flow and the temptation is strong to stretch the rules. The will to win creates temporary (at least) insanity. It causes Kevin McHale to play in the '87 NBA Finals with a broken foot, knowing he is shortening his career. It causes Washington Senators pitcher Tom Cheney to pitch 16 innings (228 pitches!) in one game, even though he isn't getting overtime. It causes Dallas Cowboys TE Jason Witten to keep running for the end zone after his helmet comes off, despite being pursued by a 260-pound Eagles linebacker who's in a cannibal club.

The primitive urge to win also causes many athletes, pro and amateur, to not only walk the fine line between honesty and larceny, but to sometimes swan dive off that fine line and wallow in Rosie Ruizville.

But what's amazing is they do it without shame! I once heard an Argentinean explain why Diego Maradona's Hand of God goal to win the 1986 World Cup (see page 156) wasn't cheating. "Tricking the referee is all part of the game," he said. *Ohhhhhhh.*

And thus, this fascinating little book. With diagrams, no less.

Still, I'm stunned that bowlers cheat. It's bowling, people!

Now if you'll excuse me, I have to go cork my Big Bertha.

7

INTRODUCTION

WHEN I CONSIDER LIFE, 'TIS ALL A CHEAT...
—John Dryden

NEVER GIVE A SUCKER AN EVEN BREAK.
—W. C. Fields

Please don't tell my mom I wrote this book.

I don't want her to think her first son is a cheater, and he's not. I have never cheated in sports, unless you count letting my sons beat me in sports when they were tots. Yes, I dumped games, like those World Series–tanking 1919 Black Sox, but I was helping my children build self-esteem. Somewhere down the line they're going to return the favor.

So why did I, a noncheater, write a book about cheating in sports?

For the adventure. It's been fun to explore a universal behavior that affects us all but isn't talked about much until the cookie jar lid slams down on some poor sap's hand. Cheating is everywhere. As Madge the Manicurist said to her shocked customer in that old TV commercial for dish soap, "You're soaking in it!"

I did not find a sport free of cheating. Chess? Lousy with cheaters, at the highest levels. Yachting, rowing, lacrosse, bowling? You bet. Maybe cheating in so-called gentlemanly sports isn't "cricket," but there is even cheating in cricket.

It's not like I was picking at a scab on sports. Cheating goes right down to the bone. We were dealing with a core issue, and most people got that, so the interviews were fun. Asking people to talk about cheating is like asking them to talk about sex. Some find the subject uncomfortable or distasteful; others simply are not dialed in to that universe. But most people jumped right in. Hall of Famers, journeymen, high school coaches—almost everyone happily shared stories (and asked what others had offered).

Few interview subjects expressed moral misgivings about cheating. Jim Palmer, the great Baltimore Orioles pitcher, told me he tried cheating only once, as a lark, unsuccessfully sandpapering a ball. But he enthusiastically told tales of cheating by others, including spitballer Gaylord Perry, and didn't seem to feel that he had been cheated by the cheaters who probably cheated him out of many victories.

"I certainly don't begrudge Gaylord," Palmer said. "For me, cheating would have ruined the quest. That sounds like it's holier-than-thou, but for me it went pretty well the way I was doing it [without cheating]."

While I was receiving cheat confessions, I never sensed shame or regret, which is probably because cheating is genetically ingrained, an extension of the competitive nature of man. The earliest sports with rules were often battles to the death, where cheating might save your life. With some athletes I interviewed, I got the sense they believe it's dishonorable, dumb, or unmanly *not* to cheat.

Because this book is likely to spark philosophical debate, here are a few starter questions: If one player is a "cheater" and another player "will do whatever it takes to win," aren't they basically the same guy? Does cheating cheapen a sport, or does it place a premium on cleverness, a basic human survival skill?

And if cheating isn't honorable, why do we honor our greatest cheaters? Gaylord Perry is in the Baseball Hall of Fame. So is Leo Durocher, who as manager would cheat rookies out of their money in card games. Utah Jazz point guard John Stockton, he of alleged illegal picks and jabby elbows and flops, will be a Hall of Famer one day. St. Louis Cardinals offensive lineman Conrad Dobler achieved folk-hero status and best-selling author-hood for his dirty tricks in pileups. Linebacker Bill Romanowski parlayed his cheap-shot infamy with four NFL teams into Super Bowl glory and a postfootball career in movies.

Cheating goes back to the dawn of time. When wife-hunting was a sport, caveguys probably corked their clubs. The first flopper was probably a Roman gladiator hoping to be taken for dead and dragged out of the arena before the emperor gave his final thumbs-down.

Maybe you've heard how pure the ancient Olympics were. Baloney. There was plenty of cheating back then, even chemical cheating. For ancient Olympians, performance-enhancing supplements included hallucinogenic mushrooms (to help the athlete get into a zone) and sheep testicles (to boost testosterone). Say, maybe that's why athletes caught cheating are often said to feel "sheepish."

(Much modern sports cheating is chemical in nature, and while I've tried to cover a wide range of sports and cheating styles in this book, you'll notice that I avoid steroids and other chemicals. The idea was to omit tips that are potentially harmful.)

If you're looking for ways to cheat, here they are. If you're merely curious about what happens on the dark side, enjoy. Maybe you want to learn what the bad guys are doing so you can counter them, in your honest way. Good for you. Best of luck. Pack a lunch.

Regardless, I salute you for your quest for deeper knowledge, as long as you don't cheat me out of my royalty by shoplifting this book. Enjoy your new knowledge and insight! And remember, not a word to my mom. She already kicks my butt in bowling, and the last thing I need is for her to see page 146.

15:21

QUARTER

4

YARDS

13

1 CH.

FOOTBALL

IN MOST SPORTS, YOU CHEAT TO GAIN AN EDGE. IN FOOTBALL, YOU CHEAT TO SURVIVE.

It's Darwinism, the law of the jungle. If your opponent gains a huge advantage by cheating and you don't counter or even beat him to the punch, you could, as someone once said, get seriously killed. Or at least lose your job.

"I cheat on every play, and so does every player I face," one veteran NFL linebacker and special-teams player says. "On special teams, when I'm the gunner, I get held every single time, and it's never called. Never. Kickoffs and punts are just a melee. Every rule is broken."

Every NFL game is officiated by a seven-man crew—referee, umpire, head linesman, line judge, field judge, side judge, and back judge. But each play is a high-speed mass collision involving twenty-two angry people. What looks like an orderly play in the playbook usually winds up looking like a chaotic jailbreak.

The rewards are high for cheating in football. If you cheat in basketball, the reward might be two points out of your team's total of one hundred. If you cheat in football and the result is a touchdown, that one play could account for half your team's scoring—it might be all you need.

When a player is penalized for holding on a touchdown, the announcers always point out that the penalty cost the holder's team a touchdown, but they never point out that the touchdown probably wouldn't have even been possible without the illegal hold.

Football is a no-excuses sport. Every play of every game is broken down and hyperanalyzed in the film room by coaches, and if you're getting beaten regularly and your coach points it out, "But that guy's cheating" is never an acceptable response.

Similarly, in a film review session, few coaches will replay you beating your man and say, "Sure, you kept him out, but I'm not sure what you're doing there is legal."

The only rule you must obey is the one expressed by Larry the Cable Guy: "Get 'er done."

HOW TO LOSE A DEFENSIVE BACK

Defensive backs can be very sticky. When they stick to a wide receiver, it's very hard for the wide receiver to catch passes. The task becomes easier if the DB is a step behind, or, better yet, does a face-plant into the turf.

"I had a habit of tripping guys," says Tim Brown, who won a Heisman Trophy at Notre Dame in 1987 and racked up 14,934 receiving yards and 100 touchdown catches in 16 NFL seasons, 15 with the Raiders. "If I had a guy running side by side with me, I would throw my foot out and the guy would trip over my leg."

The first time Brown tripped a defender, it was an accident. "[Pittsburgh Steelers cornerback] Rod Woodson was covering me. I came off the line and had to make a quick move. I stuck my leg out to plant, and he tripped over it. I realized, *Hmmm*, and I started to work on it.

"If someone said anything, I'd say, 'What do you mean? I was running a route! How can I trip you when I'm running a route?' I don't think anyone ever knew what I was doing.

"It takes time to get it down. I got called for holding all the time, but I never got called for tripping. I got pretty good at it, and guys realized they couldn't run beside me. So they'd try to stay over the top of me, or underneath, and that worked out to my advantage."

The Cheat

1 Run your route.

2 As you make your cut, plant your outside foot in front of the defensive back.

3 Push off the plant foot and cut away from the defender. With most of your weight on that foot, the leg will form a solid speed bump.

4 With the defender stumbling, catch the ball.

19 FOOTBALL

"Now the defensive backs are afraid of stumbling, and they can't play me the way they want to," Brown says, "and I can go either way. They want to stay on your hip and go with you whatever move you make, but I was able to take that away from them."

HOW TO WIN A JUMP BALL

It gets crowded in the corner of the end zone when you're trying to catch a pass. The end line and sideline hem you in, and the defender is breathing last night's dinner down your neck as you fade into that tight little corner.

"It's a jump ball," says Ken Margerum, an NFL wide receiver from 1981 to 1987. He played for the San Francisco 49ers and earned a Super Bowl championship ring with the 1985 Chicago Bears. When you're only 6 feet tall and 175 pounds, you can use some help in a jump ball situation.

The Cheat

1 Hold your body solid vertically against the defensive back's hips and shoulders.

2 When the pass is about three-fourths of the way to you, just as the defender turns his head to see the ball, jump and push off with your inside arm, hip, and elbow all at once.

The arm motion is like a quick boxing shot, only you don't fully extend your arm, just a quick elbow flip.

3 To deny the defensive back an opportunity to use this cheat's counter—which is to grab the lower part of your jersey and hinder your lift-off—make sure you elevate before he can grab.

"I used this move a lot at Stanford," says Margerum, who was an All-American. "With [quarterback] John Elway, we ran a lot of post-corner routes. This helped me get my air space."

HOW TO SET A PICK

You're a wide receiver and those annoying DBs just won't give you room to operate. It's third-and-short, man coverage. What's a guy to do? Ken Margerum, who is now an assistant coach at San Jose State, favors a play that is borrowed from basketball (where it's legal)—the screen, or pick, where one player removes his teammate's defender. The 49ers called this the "Red Left Slot Spring Right Option."

The Cheat

1 You line up at wide receiver right, with another receiver lined up in the slot eight yards off your left shoulder.

2 On the snap, you give a brief stutter-step delay, then run straight out. Your slot man runs three yards and makes a right-angle cut. As he runs just under you, you "accidentally" bump into the defensive back guarding him. Your teammate uses the pick and runs free toward the right sideline. The quarterback is sprinting right and hits the open man three yards deep.

The ref doesn't throw the flag at you for an illegal screen. Why not? Because at the moment of collision you've got your head turned toward the quarterback, your arms are up, and you're yelling for the ball, so obviously you didn't nail that guy intentionally. It's called acting.

Note: The defense will get wise. They'll see the pick coming, and they'll switch, with the guy guarding you switching to pick up the crossing slot back. When that happens, you break off your route and veer right, losing the DB who is trying to switch onto you.

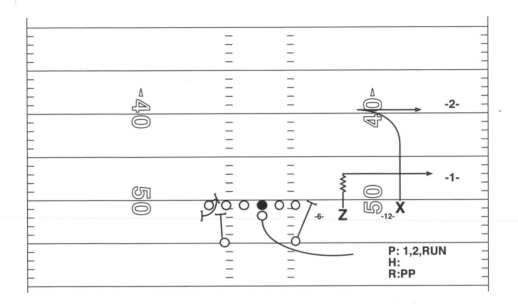

If the X man's route looks familiar, it's because this is the play that launched the 49ers dynasty. The 49ers ran the play in the 1982 NFC championship game against the Dallas Cowboys. The X man was Dwight Clark. The Z was Freddie Solomon, who was QB Joe Montana's No. 1 option. But the Cowboys defended Solomon, so Montana, rolling right, threw to his second option, Clark, crossing the end zone left to right, and Clark made "The Catch." The 49ers won the game and then the Super Bowl.

HOW TO REPEL PESKY JERSEY-GRABBERS

Football players are friendly folks; they love to hold on to one another. In big-time football there is holding on every play, sometimes by every player on the offensive line (holding, within limits, is legal for offensive linemen).

When your opponent has a grip on your jersey, he can treat you like an airport luggage handler treats a suitcase. What to do? Slime up.

Using slippery foreign substances on your jersey is illegal. Bill Romanowski, the only linebacker to start in five Super Bowls, found a way around the rule: Don't get caught. It's a costly violation. An NFL player caught with gunk on his jersey can cost his team a $50,000 fine. At lower levels, enforcement is less stringent. Know your slime police!

Cheat A (for small college and below)

Buy a can of no-stick cooking spray, the kind you use to keep your omelet from sticking to the pan. In the privacy of the locker room, spray it liberally on your buddy's jersey, then have him spray yours.

"Every Sunday after warm-ups, our defensive line would go into the shower room and spray each other," says Harris Barton, former All-Pro offensive tackle for the San Francisco 49ers.

25 FOOTBALL

"Other teams were doing it, too, but we couldn't complain to the refs because if we did they would bust our guys, too."

Bonus benefit: Tight end Brent Jones, another former 49er All-Pro and favorite target of Joe Montana and Steve Young, says, "For a receiver, there's nothing worse than getting silicone on your hands from grabbing a guy's jersey."

Cheat B (advanced method)

Bill Romanowski, NFL linebacker from 1988 to 2003 and the author of *Romo: My Life on the Edge*, says, "Early in my career they didn't check us for slimed jerseys. They didn't start checking for that stuff until about '99. I kept using it, a combination of spray and Vaseline, but you have to be very careful to apply it only to certain areas. I'd apply the Vaseline with fingertips or a Q-tip. I'd put it on the shoulder blade area and the deltoid area of the jersey. And I'd spray the front of the jersey. I never got caught, but usually they only checked the linemen."

HOW TO STAY WITH A FASTER GUY

Bill Romanowski wasn't known for his speed when he started 243 consecutive games for the San Francisco 49ers, Philadelphia Eagles, Denver Broncos, and Oakland Raiders, but if he hadn't kept up with faster offensive players, he never would have lasted sixteen NFL seasons.

The Cheat

"When you [the linebacker] are running down the field with a tight end or a running back on a pass route, you hold their pants," Romanowski says. "Not their jersey—you don't want to get caught. If you can't get a grip on the pants, hold the jersey low, down where they tuck it in."

HOW TO BE A SHUTDOWN CORNERBACK

Wide receivers can be elusive. If you're trying to guard one of them, find a handle. They all have one. It's called "shoulder pads."

The Cheat

1 In bump-and-run coverage, jam the receiver five yards or so off the line.

2 Holding both your hands as close to your chest as possible, jam your hands under the front bottom of the receiver's shoulder pads, grab the pads, and hold on.

"Everybody on Kansas City did it," says Tim Brown, the former Raider who is No. 2 on the NFL's all-time receiving-yardage list. "Denver had Ray Crockett and James Hasty; they were the best. They were strong enough that they could grab you and just make you stop in your tracks."

After a year or so Brown started taping down his jersey to his pads, using double-sided carpet tape. "So there was nothing for them to grab on to jerk," he says.

29

LORE—
Making the Cut

HOW TO CHEAT IN SPORTS

WHEN IT'S ROSTER-TRIMMING TIME IN NFL TRAINING CAMP, PANIC SETS IN. FRINGE PLAYERS WILL DO ANYTHING TO MAKE THE TEAM.

By NFL rule, an injured player can't be waived.

"Guys who thought they were going to get cut would try to hurt themselves," says a former NFL player. "They would slam their hand or arm with their locker door, and try to break a bone. It happened all the time."

Sneaky? Sure, but that kind of stuff cuts both ways in the NFL. Not uncommonly, when team A is going to play team B, team A will sign a player recently cut by team B, pump that player for information about team B, then cut the player.

Another team tactic: Place player A on the injured list to make room for player B, even though player A isn't really injured. A former NFL star tells the story of a quarterback teammate we'll call Bill.

"The team doctor told Bill, 'Your knee looks really bad. It's going to require surgery.' Bill said, 'Why do you say that?' The doctor said, 'It's obvious from the MRI.' Bill said, 'I've never had an MRI.'"

31

OVERTIME—You can't talk about cheating in football without talking about Al Davis, not that the boss of the Oakland Raiders has ever been caught cheating. But he has cunningly cultivated the persona of a James Bond–type villain, and football rivals are convinced Al is sucking secrets out of them with a nuclear vacuum cleaner. When Weeb Ewbanks coached the New York Jets of the old AFL, he would halt practice sessions every time a helicopter flew near the field, saying, "Al Davis has someone watching." Coach Harland Svare of the San Diego Chargers was even more paranoid. He once stopped in the middle of a pregame team meeting to scream at a ceiling light fixture, "Al Davis, I know you're up there!" Davis later said, "I'll tell you this: The thing wasn't in the light fixture."

—When someone came up with the idea of pumping footballs with helium to make punts fly farther, one of the first suspects was, unsurprisingly, Raiders punter Ray Guy. Studies show that, in fact, helium won't help a punter, but punters and placekickers have been known to shave or sandpaper footballs to make them

HOW TO CHEAT IN SPORTS

lighter, and to inflate or deflate balls to above or below weight specs. The league caught on and, in 1999, introduced the K-ball rule. Kicking balls are the same as regulation game balls, except that they are taken right out of the factory-sealed box by the game refs and handled only by ballboys wearing vests with a large "K."

—Spy paranoia does exist in other sports (see: Pat Riley, basketball, page 70), but nothing like what's seen in football. The late coach George Allen, who led the Los Angeles Rams and Washington Redskins, is the founding father of pigskin paranoia. When his team was practicing, every tree and tall building was seen as a probable nest for enemy spies. Allen even hired a retired cop and titled him "super security guard."

—Paying secret bonuses to NFL players is technically cheating, but you have to be able to prove it. In 1989, Buddy Ryan's Philadelphia Eagles beat the Cowboys in Dallas in a game now known as the Bounty Bowl. The Eagles knocked Cowboys place-kicker Luis Zendejas out of the game with a concussion on the opening kickoff. Cowboys coach Jimmy

Johnson accused Ryan of placing a cash bounty on the heads of Zendejas and Dallas quarterback Troy Aikman, although an NFL investigation came up empty.

—Cheating isn't always confined to the playing field. In the early '80s, the San Francisco 49ers were trying to sign a free-agent pass rusher. To close the deal, a 49ers official offered to throw in a fifty-dollar bonus for every sack. Asked the player, "Does my wife have to know about it?"

—Linebacker Bill Romanowski never met an ethical line he wouldn't cross. His use of no-stick cooking spray (see page 24) was the least of his sins. He admitted to using steroids and Human Growth Hormone. He intentionally kicked one opponent in the head and, at the bottom of a pileup, snapped a running back's finger in half. In one season, Romo was fined for three illegal hits and a punch, and for throwing a football at an opponent's crotch. In an interview for this book, Romanowski advised, "If there's going to be a fight, make sure you get in the first punch." And he walked the walk. Romo once punched a teammate in the face and knocked him out of football.

—In cold blood: Patriots fans will always have a warm spot in their hearts for Mark Henderson, a convicted burglar on a work-release program who was on the field crew for a 1982 Dolphins-Patriots game in Foxboro during a snowstorm. Late in the fourth quarter of the scoreless tie, the Pats called time to set up a thirty-three-yard field-goal attempt, a high-risk kick in the ankle-deep snow. Henderson hopped onto a snow-sweeper and cleared a stripe across the field to give kicker John Smith a launching pad for the game-winning boot.

—Is that a playbook in your pocket? In 1996, a female fan in Green Bay hit up 49ers consultant Bill Walsh for an autograph in a hotel the day before a game. Somehow the woman came away not only with an autograph but also with the top-secret script for the 49ers' first sixteen offensive plays. Credit Walsh with a fumble and the woman with an assist. She offered the info to the Packers, who later claimed they declined it. But they stopped the 49ers' offense early, and won 23–20 in overtime.

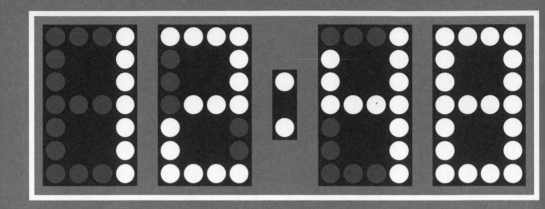

PERIOD — HOME

FOULS

CH. 2

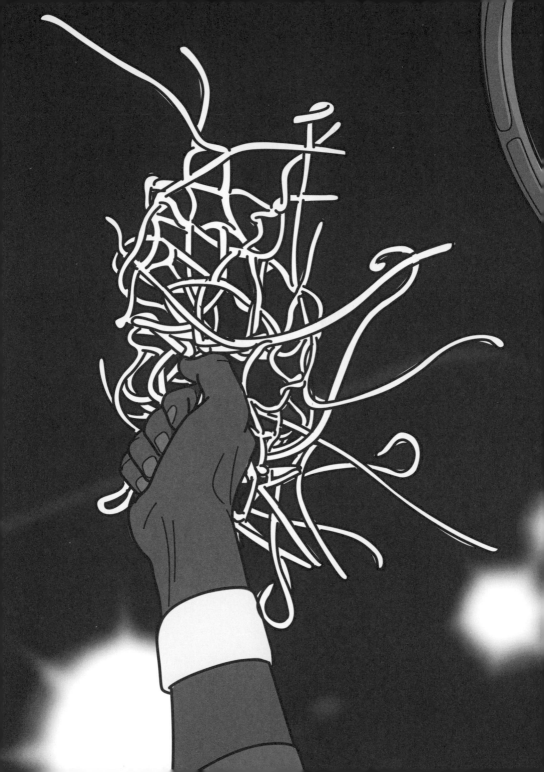

BASKETBALL

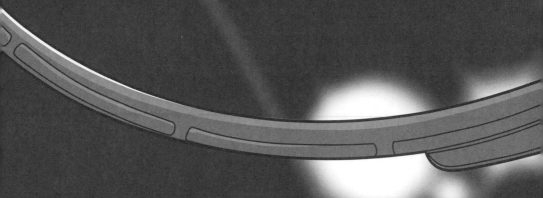

Charles Barkley was speaking for most right-thinking people in basketball when he said, "One thing I hated was when a guy went up under you [slipping his foot under yours when you were jumping for a shot] and tried to sprain your ankle, then acted like he's trying to play defense. I fucking hated their asses."

IF THERE'S ONE THING THIS BOOK STANDS FOR, IT'S HONORABLE CHEATING. INJURY-FREE CHEATING.

Not to single one guy out, but why not start at the top? The NBA's best team over the first decade of the 21st century has been the San Antonio Spurs, and their defensive stopper is Bruce Bowen, who was voted to the All-Defensive First or Second Teams seven times.

Bowen has been called a dirty player. But is he dirty or just hard-nosed? As Casey Stengel used to say, "You could look it up." It's as if Stengel knew YouTube was coming. Look, there's Bowen on many occasions doing that foot thing Charles Barkley hates. There's Bowen kicking opponents in the back, the groin, the jaw.

The Spurs got to the NBA Finals in 2006–07 with the aid of a dangerous play in the Western Conference Finals, where the Spurs' Robert Horry bodychecked the Suns' Steve Nash into the scorer's table, an incident that led to the suspension of two key Suns players for the next game.

Less lethal is the move described by former NBA veteran power forward Tom Tolbert. "You can step on a guy's foot so he can't jump," says Tolbert. "I did that a couple of times. You get an elbow in the chops. It depends on your pain tolerance, and what you're willing to give up in order to get an edge. A couple of teeth for an offensive rebound? That's too big a price to pay."

Bob McAdoo, one of the NBA's great scoring machines, had his own dangerous move. "He'd follow through on his jump shot," said former NBA center Rich Kelley, "then he'd scratch your face with his fingernails. And you'd get the foul."

Maybe it was an unintentionally dangerous part of McAdoo's shot mechanics. Maybe.

The point is: Don't do this stuff. There are plenty of ways to cheat honorably in basketball and not kill people, as we're about to show.

HOW TO GRIND DOWN AN OPPONENT

Stopping the Big Man is one of the great challenges in basketball. From Mikan to Wilt to Shaq, a long line of high-scoring centers has made life miserable for defenders, who fight for survival.

Basketball wasn't designed as a contact sport, but nowhere is that concept more of a lie than in the deep post. One of the most aggressive and creative defenders was Olden Polynice, who played fifteen NBA seasons with the Seattle SuperSonics, Los Angeles Clippers, Detroit Pistons, Sacramento Kings, and Utah Jazz. His signature ploy was the "hipbone grind."

The Cheat

1 You are defending a player on the low post. He sets up on the right-side low block. You set up behind him, overplaying him on his right shoulder to defend against an entry pass. Your right arm is in the air in standard defensive posture. Your left hand rests on your man's right hip.

2 With your right thumb, press down hard and grind on the top point of your man's left hip.

3 Repeat as needed.

"If the guy is weak-minded or ticklish, he'll react, slap your hand, get called for a foul," says Polynice. "If he's not weak-minded and doesn't react, after a while his hip gets sore and he's not as quick late in the game."

Sidebar: More Tips from a Master of Defense

Much of Olden Polynice's game was psychological.

"That's what it's about, getting into their heads," he says. "I knew how to do that; I learned it from guys like [Detroit Pistons center] Bill Laimbeer. He would manipulate your mind, make you doubt yourself. Guys assumed I was going to beat 'em up. I built that reputation early in my career. Now the legend is in place and they've got it in their mind that I might knock them out. The weak-minded players were the ones we went after. There were certain guys I could mess with. I couldn't do that with Magic Johnson. And Michael Jordan? Impossible, he was on another level. But a lot of guys . . ."

Two Polynice tricks:

- When a play is blown dead, occasionally you'll see the player with the ball take a "practice" shot. "Sometimes he does that because he's having a bad shooting night and he's taking that shot to try to find his groove," Polynice says. "[Seattle SuperSonics then-coach] Bernie Bickerstaff told us to jump up and knock that shot away. Don't give the guy a chance to get his confidence back."

- You're sitting on the bench and an opponent is standing directly in front of you, inbounding the ball. "You tug on his shorts," Polynice says. "Now you've got him looking back at your bench instead of at the game."

HOW TO DRAW
A PUSHING FOUL

Sometimes, falling down on the job is the way to go. If the ref believes you were pushed, so much the better. Grab a jersey and join the fun.

Cheat A

1 You're standing beside an opponent, battling him for rebound position. Both of you have your arms raised, your right arm crossing his left arm, behind it.

2 Raise your right arm over his arm, then lower yours over his, locking his arm against your body by pulling your arm close to your chest.

3 With a forceful pull, fall/stagger backward, yelling in pain.

Cheat B

1 The opposing team has the ball out from out-of-bounds under its own basket. You are face-guarding your man, with your back to the inbounder.

2 Get kissing-close to your man.

3 With both hands, grab one of his arms or his jersey and, keeping your arms close to your chest, fall/stagger backward, pulling him onto you. Yell.

Tom Tolbert, who played seven NBA seasons with the Charlotte Hornets, Golden State Warriors, Orlando Magic, and Los Angeles Clippers, describes how Paul Pressey, small forward for the Milwaukee Bucks, got him once: "He drove down the middle of the lane; I reached in to try to get the ball. With his off arm he trapped my arm underneath his wing, then he jumped and shot. He had my arm tight enough that I couldn't pull it free, and he pulled me back toward him, although it looked like I was pushing him. He made the layup and got the foul call. I looked at the ref and said, 'Are you kidding me? He . . . oh, forget it, you're not going to buy it.'"

47

HOW TO FLOP LIKE A PRO

Drawing a charge is a tough, smart, and self-sacrificing play.

But if the ref doesn't blow the whistle and reward you with the call, you're no hero, you're roadkill, and your opponent has a clear path to the hoop.

So you give the ref a little help. Others may place the negative label of "flopping" on your move, but we prefer to think of it as assuring that justice is done and that hard, honest work is rewarded—as a result of acting. As Shakespeare observed, we're all actors.

People generally want to believe in the honesty of people, and you can take advantage of that weakness. Refs are a lot like people, only more gullible. Refs understand on an intellectual level that a guy like Vlade Divac (16-year NBA player for the Los Angeles Lakers, Charlotte Hornets, and Sacramento Kings) couldn't possibly get knocked down as easily and as often as he did, unless he was faking. Vlade sometimes resembled a Christmas tree without a stand.

"He's flopping" was the message the ref received from the reasoning and logic center of his brain when Vlade hit the hardwood.

But the ref's "mankind-is-good" brain center was telling him, "No, I think he really got fouled this time. Look at the anguish on his face. My god!"

And Vlade would get the call.

The flop comes in two flavors: offensive and defensive.

Offensive Flopping

You've got the ball; you drive to the hoop. You are well defended, or your shot is blocked.

Tips

- If the defender reaches in to strip the ball, use your non-dribbling arm to trap the defender's arm and pin it against your body so it looks like he's grabbing or pushing you.

- Contort your body in awkward ways to convince the ref that the defender's contact knocked you out of your poetry-in-motion move.

- Yell in pain. Even if the ref suspects that you're flopping—faking—but has responded to your theatrics by reflexively blowing his whistle, you've got a good chance to get the call. Refs don't like to look bad.

Tom Tolbert says when he played for the Golden State Warriors, coach Don Nelson had the players work on screaming in practice. "Terry Teagle would start screaming before he put the ball on the ground to make his move. Of guys in the league, Magic [Johnson] was the best at it. He'd just go to the hole and throw up a shot and scream, and the ref would put him at the line.

"I wouldn't abuse it or overuse it. But if I was driving and wound up with a bad angle, or got stuck and didn't have an outlet for a pass and had to just throw up a bad shot, I might try to jump into somebody and yell."

Offensive Flop

Defensive Flop

Defensive Flopping

The key is to make it look like you established sound defensive position and got hammered.

Tips

- Just before contact, subtly shift your weight from the balls of your feet to your heels, so you look solidly planted and stable, but you can be knocked back easily.

- While staggering backward, act as if you are trying to maintain your balance and not fall.

- Fall straight back, not at an angle, thus showing that you were positioned squarely in front of the offensive player when you were viciously attacked.

- If you fall, attempt to get as much backward butt-skid as possible.

- Flail your arms.

- Try to get a piece of the ball to prevent an easy layup in the event that the ref doesn't feel your pain.

- Use your face. Register surprise, shock, pain. Practice in front of a mirror.

- Don't "recover" too quickly after the contact. Olden Polynice says, "If I got the call, I tried not to smile; the refs look for that."

Although you just got the call, if you look smug about it, you won't get that call the next time. Remember, cheating is a marathon, not a sprint.

It helps to know your refs! "With Joey Crawford, I couldn't get away with anything," says confessed flopper Polynice. "If it was Dick Bavetta, I could get away with a flop now and then."

The flop works at any level of ball, but the higher the league, the more artful must be the act.

"It was much easier to get away with the flop in college," says Tolbert, an All-American forward at Arizona. "It was so easy in college that sometimes I felt guilty. My first NBA preseason game, Larry Nance posted me up, he barely bumped me, and I flopped to the ground. Nance turned around and laid it in, and the official looked at me and said, 'This ain't college. Get up.' I didn't realize that to get a flop foul in the NBA you had to overact like Jim Carrey, or Vlade Divac."

Sidebar: Do Refs Cheat?

"When I was playing for Orlando," says Tom Tolbert, "I got called for a foul that should have been on Shaq. I looked over at the ref and said, 'That wasn't on me, I was like two feet away, how did you call that on me?'

"The ref looked at me and said, 'Well, would you rather have Shaq with four fouls, or you with two?' I said, 'I'd rather have Shaq with four. I want to play. That foul might put me on the bench.'

"Did the ref do that on purpose? Absolutely. They know who the fans come to see, no question."

HOW TO GET A DEFENDER TO FOUL YOUR FOOT

Lloyd (later World B.) Free, who played in the NBA from 1975 to 1988, is widely credited with originating what we'll call the jump-shot kick-flop. Kick your defender while you're shooting and make it look like he made illegal contact.

The Cheat

1 As you go up for a jump shot, your defender in your face or rushing past your side, kick one foot out and make contact with the defender.

2 As the shot is released, lurch and stumble to sell the foul.

Rick Barry, Hall of Fame forward, explains how World B. Free did it: "Free would go up for a jump shot and put out his leg and kick you [the defender]. He'd make it seem like you hit him, then he'd fall down."

Bill Walton, Hall of Fame center, was also victimized by Free, adding, "Or World would stick his leg out to the side and kick you as you ran by."

Reggie Miller, shooting guard for the Indiana Pacers from 1987 to 2005, inherited Free's crown as king of the jump-shot kick-flop. Miller took a lot of perimeter shots with defenders running at him,

54

and he would kick a leg out to the side to make contact as the defender flew past; then he would react as if fouled.

NBA referees might have wised up to Reggie's trick eventually, but he played only eighteen seasons.

HOW TO SLOW DOWN A RUNNING TEAM

Your next opponent is faster than your team and likely to run you dizzy, even on made baskets.

How to nullify their speed advantage? Make 'em wait for the ball by hanging "slower" nets.

When the Loyola Marymount (Los Angeles) Lions were the highest scoring men's college team in the nation in 1989–1990, there seemed to be no way to slow them. They scored one hundred or more points an NCAA-record twenty-five times. They were effective running their break even on opponents' made baskets. With no letup, they ran foes ragged.

"When we were on the road," says Paul Westhead, then Loyola's coach, "we'd have a shootaround at the arena the night before the game or the morning of the game. After a while we noticed that every gym we went to had brand-new nets.

"We would have one of our guys stand on a chair and just stretch each net out for about twenty minutes. It became our routine."

New nets are tighter than broken-in nets, and they hold the ball, rather than let it drop through cleanly. Also, nets come in different weights. The thick ones are gluey, like spiderwebs; they trap balls. To slow down a running team, buy thick or long nets and install them the day of the game.

For extra snugging, run the nets through the laundry—hot rinse and hot dry. Don't use fabric softener, which will slicken the nets! You want the nets tight, but if they're too snug, the ball stays in the net, like in the original peach baskets. *Too* retro.

Says Tom Tolbert: "The Celtics back in about '89 had some old guys, like Dennis Johnson and Robert Parish, and they didn't want teams running back on them off their own made baskets, so they had these extra-thick nets, thicker than anything you'd see anywhere else in the league. The ball would almost swirl inside it, or sometimes it would almost pop back out, and you'd have to wait for it to come down."

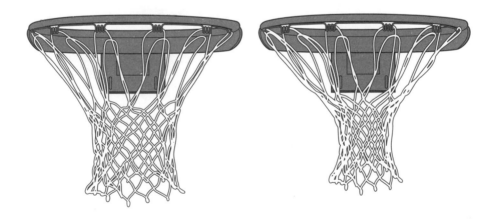

HOW TO GET YOUR OPPONENT TO CHOOSE THE WRONG BASKET

On your home court, you always have a favorite end.

The good end might have a softer rim to benefit shooters, or better lighting than the other hoop, or a dead spot in the floor that will cause dribbling problems for your foe, or spectator seating behind it so your fans can distract opposing free-throw shooters.

Generally, you want to be going to the good end in the second half, when subtle advantages can mean the difference in a close game. You're the home team, and you don't get to choose, because selection is the right of the visiting team. But you can influence your opponent's decision. Think of it as a Jedi mind trick.

Some visiting coaches instruct their team to chase the home team off whatever end they're on, regardless, as a psychological ploy or power move. Know your opposing coach. If he or she has this M.O., your task is simple—have your team come out early and warm up on the end you don't want.

More often, the visiting team needs your guidance.

Paul Westhead, who coached the Los Angeles Lakers to the NBA championship in 1980 and also coached the Phoenix Mercury to a WNBA title in 2007, began his coaching career at Cheltenham High near Philadelphia, famous as Reggie Jackson's high school.

Behind one basket in the Cheltenham gym is a large window. During afternoon games, the sun shines through the window and into the eyes of shooters. But by the second half, the sun is low and no longer a factor. Westhead's boys wanted the nonwindow end of the court for the first half.

"We would come out early so we'd be shooting around on the good end when the visiting team came out," Westhead says.

"A lot of times, the other team would just take the end of the court that's not being used. But after a while, the other teams figured out what we were doing, so they'd chase us off the good end.

"So we started staying in the locker room longer, letting the visiting team come out first. I would arrange for three or four guys from the previous gym class to stay on the good end of the court and just shoot around. When the visiting team came out, they would tend to take the other end, rather than go to the hassle of asking the gym kids to leave."

Sometimes, what makes one end of the court favorable is a factor that can be changed at halftime. Small college and high school gyms, especially, have quirks that can be exploited. Look around. Be creative.

When NBA scout and TV analyst Dave Bollwinkel was a high school coach, his home gym had a theater stage behind one basket. The stage had a large curtain. When the curtain was open, the open space adversely affected the depth perception of shooters, in much the same way that courts inside domed stadiums tend to be shooter-unfriendly.

"At halftime," Bollwinkel says, "we'd have our student manager open or close the curtains, depending on which way we were going."

HOW TO SWAP IDENTITIES

In the old days, until the early 1980s, a player who was called for a foul was required to raise his or her hand, to indicate to the official scorer who the foul was on.

The rule is gone, but an opportunity remains. Take a foul that belongs to your more-valuable teammate.

The Cheat

The ref calls a foul on your teammate Joe. Joe averages twenty points a game, and he's already got three fouls. Your team can't afford to lose Joe. You are a team player, so you position yourself near Joe immediately after the call and quickly raise your hand and try to make eye contact with the official scorer. With luck, the scorer will credit you with the foul, even when the ref signals Joe's jersey number. Scorers are human.

This won't work in the NBA or in major college ball. The lower the level of ball, the more likely you'll get away with it.

If you're caught in the act, you simply plead innocent. Hey, you thought the ref called the foul on you—you were just being honest.

Variation: Your teammate Bill is fouled while shooting and will go to the line for a pair of free throws. But Bill is a 30 percent free-throw shooter. You shoot 75 percent. In the pre-free-throw huddle, you tell Bill, "I'll take 'em." And you go to the line and shoot the pair.

Caution: This one is riskier; you could get yourself a T.

LORE—
The Big Bang

On free throws, standard procedure is for the player with the low spot along the lane to step in front of the player next to him and block him off the boards. Basic basketball. Slam dancing, however, is illegal.

Rich Kelley, who played center for seven NBA teams over eleven seasons, tells of his welcome-to-the-NBA moment.

The Boston Celtics were in New Orleans playing Kelley's Jazz. A Celtic was shooting a free throw, so Kelley had the inside spot on the right side of the lane; Boston center Dave Cowens lined up to Rich's left.

"But instead of standing right next to me," Kelley says, "Cowens moved as far left as he could, away from me."

"WHEN THE SHOT WENT UP AND I TRIED TO STEP TO MY LEFT TO CUT HIM OFF, HE TOOK A RUNNING START AND JUST CREAMED ME."

Kelley is no wuss, and he went to Stanford, so he's no dummy.

"I decided I could do that, too. Next free throw, he's way away to my left again, so I move as far as I can to my right. He wants to bang, I'll bang. The shot goes up, I take a lunge at him, he side-steps me, and I fall down and slide all the way to the free-throw line on my ass."

63

HOW TO WIN A JUMP BALL AGAINST A TALLER FOE

Want to win that jump? A coach explains how:

> "Jump early. It's illegal, but the worst thing that can happen is the ref gives the other team the ball out of bounds. The risk-reward ratio is good. But don't jump into the guy, because that gets called."

HOW TO EXTEND YOUR SCREEN

A veteran college coach offers two tips on making your screen more effective.

- When you set a screen but the man you're trying to screen slips through the screen in front of you, slide-step backward, giving your teammate a second chance to use your screen. Refs are looking for illegal side movement by the screener and seldom call movement straight back.

- If the defender slips the screen by going behind you, pivot toward the basket with your hands up, as if you're looking for a pass, and accidentally bump the defender.

A former NBA star adds, "Stagger back to make it look like the defensive guy banged into you."

We'll call that a pick flop.

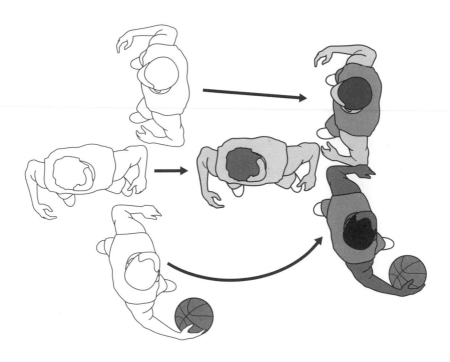

HOW TO ADJUST THE RIMS

It's the home team's obligation to make sure the rims are "properly" adjusted. Depending on the type of shooters you have, and the type the other team has, your team will benefit from either looser or tighter rims.

If you're playing a high-scoring, good-shooting team, especially a perimeter-shooting team, stiff rims will tend to lower its shooting percentage.

Conversely, if you are the outside-shooting team, or you're playing a slow and defensive-minded team, looser rims will increase scoring and diminish their advantage.

The Cheat

1 Get a ladder and a crescent wrench.

2 Climb.

3 Adjust the tension bolt housed inside the triangular casing between the rim and the backboard. In some cases, backboard supports and support wires can be snugged or loosened, too.

4 Test. Remember, you're trying to achieve subtle changes in rim tension, nothing dramatic or obvious.

Note: Normally you'll do the adjusting in an empty gym long before the game. However, it's not unusual for a janitor to bring out a ladder and make adjustments or repairs at halftime. If a ref inquires, an honest explanation would be "There seems to be something loose up there."

Different styles and models of rims have different bounce characteristics. Consider owning two sets of rims and changing them as the situation dictates.

HOW TO FOUL A SHOOTER WITHOUT GETTING CAUGHT

Rick Barry played fourteen seasons of professional basketball, in the NBA and ABA, and in four of those seasons he averaged more than thirty points. If defenders hadn't fouled him on nearly every shot attempt and gotten away with most of those fouls, the man might have destroyed the game with his greatness. The art was in fouling Barry (or any shooter) and getting away with it.

The Cheat

1 When your man goes up for a jump shot, you go up with him.

2 Raise one arm straight up to challenge the shot.

3 With the other arm, stealthily jab or push the shooter in his shooting elbow, midsection, or leg. Strike like a cobra.

"It would drive me nuts; guys would kind of touch your elbow," Barry says. "Or, more subtle, they would push your leg a bit, push it to the side, and that tiny nudge is going to throw off the shooter's body.

"I'd go ballistic when officials would say, 'Hey, he never touched you.'"

Note: When nobody was guarding or fouling him—at the free-throw line—Barry shot 90 percent for his NBA career.

OVERTIME—Although they never had to worry about it, opposing coaches surely would have screamed that this was cheating, but it wasn't: When Wilt Chamberlain was a freshman at the University of Kansas, during practice he would sometimes shoot free throws by stepping back to just inside the top of the free-throw circle, taking one or two quick steps forward, leaping from behind the free-throw line like a long jumper, soaring through the air, and dunking his free throw. Technically it was legal, but word spread throughout basketball and the rulesmakers quickly passed a rule, still on the books: "The free-throw shooter may not cross the plane of the free-throw line until the . . . free throw ends."

—Spying in basketball? Happens all the time, and it's high on the fear list of most coaches. College teams routinely close practices, chasing out even students hoping to watch, because who knows which student might be a spy?

—In the NBA, Pat Riley is a paranoia pioneer, taking fear of spying to a new level. These days NBA practices are almost always closed to the media, but

HOW TO CHEAT IN SPORTS

Riley, when he was coach of the Lakers from 1981–90, was among the first NBA coaches to adopt this practice. He referred to newspaper, radio, and TV people as "the peripheral enemy." But he didn't stop with the media. During the 1984 Lakers vs. Celtics NBA Finals at the old Boston Garden, Riley had security personnel clear out the cleaning crew before a practice, including an elderly woman mopping the floor. On another occasion in Boston, Riley ordered the Lakers' courtside water supply to be dumped, fearing that Celtics President Red Auerbach had spiked it.

—That news no doubt made old Red very happy, because nobody ever reveled in a reputation for playing devious mind games more than him. It was as if he believed the Celtics' nine NBA championships during his coaching reign were as much due to his psychological tactics as to his coaching and to the presence of great players like Bill Russell. "In the old Boston Garden in the summer, the visitors' locker room was always ten to fifteen degrees hotter than the rest of the building," said Paul Westhead, coach of the Lakers from 1979–81. "You'd come out of the locker room and your players would be almost in a stupor." Cold showers and clogged toilets were also in Red's bag o' tricks.

— Ouch: In one of the more widely replayed (and non-called) fouls in recent NBA seasons, Denver Nuggets forward Reggie Evans, boxed off the boards by Clippers center Chris Kaman on a rebound play, reached between Kaman's legs, grabbed his jock and its contents, and gave them a good yank. "He tried to rip 'em off, basically," Kaman said.

— "There's a lot of grabbing of shorts, grabbing of shirts in the NBA," said Tom Tolbert, survivor/agitator of seven NBA seasons. "Kevin McHale, I'd be running down the court on the break, I'd be ahead of him, and he'd just grab my shirt and tug me. I'm like, 'Come on, dude, keep up! I'm only averaging 8 or 9 points, I'm trying to get down there and get a layup, let me go!'"

— Rick Barry, famed for his shooting, also had other skills. He knew how to box guys off the boards. Well, some guys. "[Former Washington Bullets center] Wes Unseld," Barry recalled, "you'd have him screened off the boards, he'd put both his hands in the air like

he's going for the rebound, then with those big power-
ful legs, he'd just kind of walk you out of the way,
just move you forward. His hands are up in the air and
he's killing you with his legs. All of a sudden you're
under the basket."

—The most effective way to cheat in college basketball is by illegal recruiting, including improper induce-
ments to players and recruits. Jerry Tarkanian (UNLV
coach, 1973–92) was considered by many to be the
poster boy for anything-goes recruiting, though he
and his programs were never actually caught. In one
famous incident, a Las Vegas newspaper printed
a photo of three players from UNLV's 1990 national
championship team relaxing in a backyard hot tub
with Richard "The Fixer" Perry, convicted earlier for
his part in a college gambling scheme. Tarkanian
clearly wasn't looking for scholars. When he was
coaching at Long Beach State, one day two of his
players were sharing a cab with a sportswriter. The
discussion turned to politics. "Who's the President
[of the U.S.]?" one player asked. The other replied,
"I don't know, but he's doing a lousy job."

Tired of long beer lines at the concession booth? Find the side door used by the beer vendor and get a cold one before he makes his rounds in the stands.

1	2	3	4	5	6	7	8	9
0	1	2	0					
1	3	0	1					

BALL   **STRIKE**

0   0

R H E

3 6 1

5 4 0

OUT

0

CH.

Baseball is the only sport that presents its philosophy of cheating in a motto, which is presented to every big leaguer during his unofficial rookie orientation:

"IF YOU AIN'T CHEATIN', YOU AIN'T TRYIN'."

In no other sport is cheating considered as romantic or noble as it is in baseball, and that probably goes back to the roots of the game. In the early days, professional ballplayers weren't considered heroic figures, but rather were seen as uncouth ruffians who played baseball in order to avoid honest work.

While golf and tennis were governed by strong honor systems, baseball developed an honor system similar to that of pickpocketing—you're guilty only if you're caught. And you certainly never turn yourself in.

Now baseball players are the crème of society, but the sport has never lost its original ragged edges. It's still the only game in which players chew and spit tobacco and scratch and adjust certain body parts during live action. The first pitcher to throw a spitball probably did so after accidentally drooling tobacco juice onto the ball or blowing his nose into his glove.

Those early ballplayers would be proud to see that players today are still cheatin' their hearts out. They would be especially proud of Dave Bresnahan, a catcher for the Double-A Williamsport Bills in 1987.

In a moment of creative whimsy, Bresnahan peeled a raw potato and hid it in the dugout. When the situation was right—a runner on third—Bresnahan called time, went to the dugout, covertly fetched the potato and hid it in his glove. After catching the next pitch, Bresnahan threw the potato into left field on a "wild" pickoff attempt. The runner trotted home, only to be tagged out with the real ball.

Bresnahan was released by the Cleveland Indians' organization for "jeopardizing the integrity of the game." The opposing manager enjoyed the joke and felt the punishment was too harsh, but agreed that the umps were right to toss Bresnahan out of the game.

"That potato was scuffed," the skipper said. "He definitely used a knife on it."

HOW TO CORK A BAT

A batter using a corked bat risks inspection, ejection, dejection, and suspension. Plus, there is no scientific proof that a corked bat boosts power. Still, bat corking is ingrained (so to speak) in baseball.

Ballplayers cork on, flaunting MLB Rule 6.06 (d). At least seven major leaguers have been busted with doctored bats. Sammy Sosa of the Chicago Cubs accidentally (he says) used his corked batting-practice bat in a game in June 2003. His bat splintered, and cork littered the infield. Sosa was suspended for seven games, costing him about $600,000, believed to be history's highest corkage fee.

Many players believe that if the bat barrel is hollowed out and filled with a less-dense material like cork (the filler serves mostly to prevent structural weakness and to preserve the natural sound), the ounce or two of decreased weight translates to greater swing speed (the c^2, or velocity part, of Einstein's $E = mc^2$) and thus more power. Some say the decreased density also adds whip or bend to the bat, providing a trampoline effect similar to what happens on the face of a high-tech golf driver.

The problem with this theory is that by decreasing the bat's weight in the cork-for-wood swap, you're also decreasing the weapon's mass. Since mass is the m of $E = mc^2$, a decrease in mass will offset the benefit of the increase in swing speed. Net benefit: zilch.

As for the "trampoline effect," no. Studies show no increased rebound effect in hollowed-out bats, no matter what they're stuffed with. The ball doesn't stay in contact with the bat long enough for any significant return of energy.

82

However, and pay attention here: When a bat is corked, the center of gravity is changed, giving the bat a lower "swing weight." What's important is not that the bat is lighter, but that it's lighter in the barrel. The center of gravity has been shifted closer to the hands.

Physicist Alan M. Nathan (of the University of Illinois at Urbana-Champaign*) invites you to try this simple experiment: Flip a bat over, grip it around the top of the barrel, and swing it. See, it's easier to swing!

Writes Professor Nathan, "The lighter weight [of a corked bat] and smaller swing weight also lead to better bat control, which has a beneficial effect for a contact-type hitter . . ."

It's all about control. With a corked bat, the batter can wait a fraction of a second longer before starting his swing, *and* he can make more fine adjustments during the swing. This allows the hitter to make more consistent contact with the bull's-eye center of the bat's sweet spot, where power lies. Power hitters don't stop hitting homers because they get weaker, but because they lose the quickness and control of their bat to make solid contact. Result: better hitting, but not because of added "pop" from the cork.

So a corked bat will benefit a slugger and a banjo hitter. Please don't ask us how to cork a banjo.

* See his Web site at www.npl.uiuc.edu/~a-nathan/pob

The Cheat

This recipe is provided by Dr. Cork (not his real name), who worked for a West Coast major league team during the '80s and '90s and corked bats for several players. Players claimed Dr. Cork's handiwork added five to eight feet to their drives. →

Materials

- short ¾-inch-diameter dowel (for plug)

- heavy towel or piece of heavy cloth

- standard wooden bat, preferably with cupped barrel top, natural wood color or black.

- bench vise or floor vise

- power hand drill

- standard-length ⅛-inch drill bit

- 1-foot-long ¹¹/₁₆-inch drill bit, standard tip (do not use blade-type, "wood-boring" bit, which will tend to clog)

- small bag of corks, often sold as "popgun" size (⁹/₁₆-inch top, ½ inch long)

- 1-foot-long piece of ½-inch-diameter dowel (to be used as tamping tool)

- claw hammer or rubber mallet

- bottle of Elmer's Glue-All

- sander drill bit

- slotted screwdriver or small chisel

- small can of wood stain or Verathane, tone and finish to match bat

Steps

1 Cut a 1-inch-long piece of ¾-inch dowel; set aside to use as final cap.

2 Wrap the towel or heavy cloth around the bat's barrel (to protect the wood from vise scratches) and clamp the bat into the bench vise, either horizontally in bench vise or vertically in floor vise. You can use more sophisticated tools such as a drill press to assure dead-center coring, but Dr. Cork uses a handheld power drill, relying on steady hand and sure eye.

3 With the ⅛-inch bit, drill a vertical guide hole into the top of the bat, 1½ inches deep. →

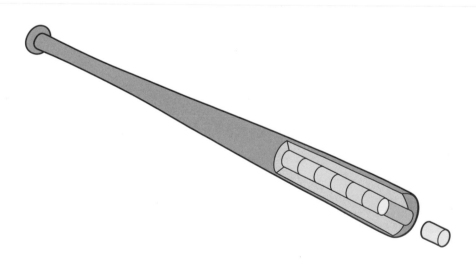

4 With the 1-foot-long ¹¹/₁₆-inch bit, drill a core hole 9–10 inches deep, or to the depth of the lightning-bolt logo on the side of a Louisville Slugger. Back the bit out frequently to avoid overheating and sawdust clogging.

5 Insert corks, one at a time, wide end first. (**Note:** Some advocate filling the hole with Super Balls, or newspaper, or leaving it empty. Dr. Cork recommends cork.) After every three corks are inserted, take the 1-foot-long piece of ½-inch dowel, insert into the hole, and tamp firmly with the hammer or mallet to "spread" and compress the corks. Tamp until there's no more give. Continue adding corks. No glue yet! Fill the corks to within one inch of the top of the hole.

6 Test the reserved 1-inch-long ¾-inch dowel plug to make sure it fits snugly into the hole, tight enough so that it has to be pushed or tapped lightly with hammer to seat it. Spread glue liberally on the sides of the dowel plug, insert the plug, and push or tap until the top of the dowel is flush with the bat surface.

7 Allow two days for glue to dry.

8 With the sander drill bit, lightly sand the top of the plug and surrounding surface.

9 With the screwdriver or small chisel, carefully carve simulated grain marks on top of the dowel plug to match the grain pattern on top of the bat (this step is not necessary with a black bat).

10 Apply a light coat of wood stain or Verathane over the entire cupped area (or top of bat, if rounded-top type). With a black bat, use matching black paint.

11 When the bat is completely dry, jam the top end into loose dirt and twist several times to give a natural "used" finish.

LORE—
Notes on a
Corkboard

In 1994, Cleveland Indians outfielder Albert Belle's bat was con-fiscated by umpires who had been tipped that Belle was using a corked bat. The umps had the bat placed in their locker room to be examined later.

With the game in progress, Indians pitcher Jason Grimsley sneaked into the umps' room through a ceiling ventilation duct, took the Belle bat, and left another bat in its place. Umpires became suspicious later when they noticed that the bat to be examined was a Paul Sorrento model. Belle was suspended for ten games (reduced to seven on appeal).

Other major leaguers busted for using a corked bat include All-Star third baseman Chris Sabo, Billy Hatcher of the Houston Astros, New York Yankees All-Star third baseman Graig Nettles, Jose Guillen of the Seattle Mariners, and Wilton Guerrero of the Los Angeles Dodgers. Suspensions ranged from seven to ten games. Nettles's bat barrel was filled with Super Balls.

HOW TO THROW A YARNBALL

The yarnball doesn't get the attention accorded its famous cousins, the scuffball and the spitball, but the yarnball is a quiet workhorse. Pitchers who pluck yarn say they get an unnaturally strong bite on their breaking ball, and this pitch flies under the radar—nobody gets busted for a yarnball.

The Cheat

1 Using a thumbnail, scratch a half-inch-long section of the ball's yarn stitching, at a point where your index finger will contact the seam. Scratch until the yarn is slightly frayed and raised.

2 Grip the ball with your usual curveball or fastball grip and, with your fingertip on the newly created ridge of frayed yarn, let 'er rip, pulling hard on the yarn as you release. The raised yarn gives your finger added traction for extra spin and ball action.

The goal is to fray and raise the yarn to improve the grip and increase an imbalance of air drag on one side of the ball.

"Raising the seam is good for the fastball and the curveball," says our expert. "Absolutely better feel. For the fastball, use the four-seam grip."

This pitch will keep you out of trouble. A former twenty-game-winning big leaguer says, "Umpires are looking for blemishes on the skin of the ball—they don't look at the seams."

Note: A similar cheat is common in cricket, where the bowler (pitcher) illegally nicks or lifts the threads or seam to achieve a large amount of "reverse swing." In a 2006 Pakistan-England match, Pakistan was penalized for tampering with the seam of the ball. The team protested by delaying its return after tea. The umpires declared a forfeit.

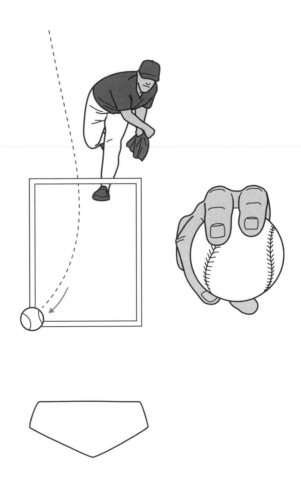

HOW TO THROW A SCUFFBALL

The baseball is designed with a slick cowhide cover that ensures a smooth and uneventful flight. But scuff happens. With enough scuff, a baseball becomes a Wiffle Ball.

The Cheat

1 Nick, scuff, or abrade a small blemish into the cowhide. Scuff tools include belt buckles, metal grommets on gloves, small patches of sandpaper superglued to the heel of the glove hand, diamond rings, thumb tacks hidden in a glove, and nail files.

2 Grip the ball like a two-seam fastball, with the scuff on the opposite side of the direction you want the ball to break. That is, if you want the ball to break left, have the scuff on the right; if you want the ball to drop, hold the scuff on top.

3 Throw your pitch and let Mother Wind Resistance take its course.

As the air flowing over the spinning ball encounters the scuff, the ball swerves. Says 1986 All-Star pitcher Mike Krukow, "You throw it like a fastball and you get the movement for free."

Baltimore Orioles Hall of Famer Jim Palmer only tried a scuffball in a game once, but he knows it can be effective.

90

"Hitters are looking for spin and velocity," he says. "The scuffball has a fastball spin, then all of a sudden it just sails. The hitter has already made up his mind, and if the ball moves, he's got no chance.

"There was a rumor that Nolan Ryan, near the end of his career, came up with a great two-seam fastball that would just dive, and everybody thought he was scuffing the ball. Phil Bradley said the Orioles were talking about Nolan scuffing the ball. I said to Phil, 'Why don't you just ask the umpire to check the ball?' He said, 'Are you crazy? Nolan would hit me in the head!'"

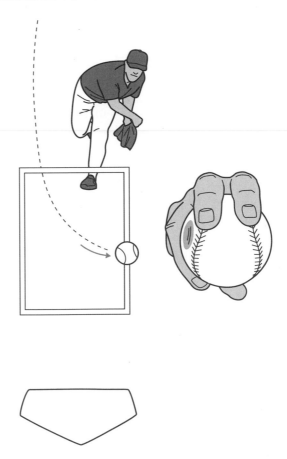

Sidebar: It Takes a Village to Scuff

The pitcher can do the nicking and scuffing, certainly, but he's the center of attention. Teammates can help.

"When the pitcher is warming up before the inning and the ball hits the dirt, the umpire will throw it out," says a former big leaguer. "But when the pitcher makes his last warmup throw and the catcher throws down to second, if the ball goes in the dirt, the umpire isn't even watching. The catcher can throw it in the dirt, or the guy taking the throw can just back up and take it on a hop behind the bag. The [now-scuffed] ball will stay in play.

"Or when the first baseman is throwing grounders to the other infielders, he can time it so he throws the second baseman a grounder right when the catcher's throw is coming down. The second baseman switches balls, and your pitcher gets one or two pitches with a tired old ball [before the ump or hitter gets wise]."

The catcher is used to doing dirty work; let him help here by nicking the ball on a shin-guard buckle, a sharpened edge of a shin guard, or his belt buckle.

93

LORE—
The Ball Sorter

In the '80s and '90s, many pitchers say, there were two distinctly different types of balls used in the major leagues, made in two different countries. One ball was slightly larger with flatter seams; the other was smaller with higher seams. The balls were intermixed. A pitcher's anonymous confession:

"One year I sat in the bullpen during games when I wasn't pitching and collected all the home-run balls hit out there. What I found was that all the balls hit there were the small balls. They were harder and they carried better than the bigger balls.

"SO WHEN IT WAS MY TURN TO PITCH, I'D GET TO THE PARK EARLY AND HANDPICK THE GAME BALLS.

"When it was my start, I'd get the boxes of game balls from the clubhouse guy and I'd sort 'em out. I'd pick out all the big balls and put 'em in the bag of that night's game balls."

Question: But didn't that benefit the opposing pitcher, also?

Pitcher: "I didn't give a shit."

HOW TO THROW A SPITBALL

The spitball was ruled illegal in 1921, but seventeen pitchers were exempted from that ban by a grandfather clause. Burleigh Grimes and sixteen other pitchers who built their careers around the spitball were allowed to load up and loogie up balls for the remainder of their big-league careers.

Apparently, some present-day pitchers believe they qualify for that grandfather amnesty. That's one possible explanation for the continued use of the spitter today. The other explanation: It works.

The spitter falls faster than a rookie batter's jaw the first time he sees one.

The Cheat

1 Wet your index and middle fingers using saliva, K-Y Jelly, petroleum jelly, slippery elm, hair oil, suntan lotion, or the wetting agent of your choice. Your product can be kept under the brim of your cap, inside your belt, on the back of your neck, somewhere on your glove, in your hair . . .

2 Grip the ball like a two-seam fastball, but with the middle and index fingers together.

3 Let your Burleigh Grimes Special fly, and leave the batters swinging at air.

"Throw it like a two-seam fastball," says Mike Krukow, who never used the pitch in a game. "That's the beauty of the spitter—you don't do anything with it and the bottom drops out. It doesn't do anything bad to your arm."

Note: When Billy Martin managed the Oakland A's, his pitchers allegedly threw Ivory Soap balls. Rub Ivory Soap powder on the outside thigh seam of your uniform pants. Wipe fingers on seam to pick up slippery soap film.

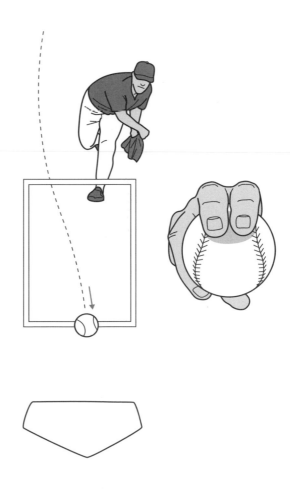

LORE—
Mr. Spit

FIVE-TIME ALL-STAR PITCHER GAYLORD PERRY'S AUTO-BIOGRAPHY IS TITLED *ME AND THE SPITTER.*

Says Duane Kuiper, former second baseman for the Cleveland Indians and San Francisco Giants, "I was a cheerful kid who loved to pick up gloves and try 'em on. My first day in the big leagues, in the dugout during batting practice, I picked up Gaylord's glove, and oh, my god! You'd'a thought I just robbed a bank. He laid into me so bad. From then on I knew the starting pitchers' gloves were off-limits."

Kuiper adds that Indians third baseman Buddy Bell "would get five errors every year when he'd throw the ball into the seats behind first base because he picked up Gaylord's loaded-up ball. Buddy said, 'How am I going to explain that if someone asks me what happened?'"

Perry used various methods to load up the ball, including two that would flunk a Board of Health inspection. He would eat red pepper to make his nose run, then use the snot to slime the ball. Or he would hide Vaseline on his zipper, assuming no ump would search there.

Jim Palmer tells this story: "Steve Stone asked Gaylord to teach him the spitter. Gaylord said, 'You got $10,000, kid?' And he was serious. In retrospect, Stoney should have done it. He wouldn't have had to throw all those curveballs to win twenty-five games [and the Cy Young Award] in '80 if he'd paid the $10,000. It would have been a bargain."

99

LORE—
Cops and Rubbers

IF SO MANY PITCHERS DOCTOR SO MANY BASEBALLS, WHY DO SO FEW OF THEM GET CAUGHT?

Because umpires don't want the job of being the K-Y cop or the sandpaper sleuth.

If the umps tried to bust every pitcher who doctors a ball, it would open up a can of worms—which a guy like Kenny Rogers might try to rub on the ball.

Rogers, pitching for the Detroit Tigers in Game 2 of the 2006 World Series, set off a controversy when TV close-ups showed a large yellow-brown hunk of gunk near the base of his left (glove hand) thumb. Rogers swore it was dirt, although TV detective work turned up proof that the random smudge was there every time Rogers pitched.

St. Louis Cardinals manager Tony LaRussa declined to demand that the umpires inspect Rogers, who escaped unpunished. Why did LaRussa cut Rogers a break? Possibly because the veteran skipper knows that many pitchers, including his own, use pine tar to improve their grip on the ball, especially in cold weather.

"When I pitched at Candlestick," says Mike Krukow, former Giants ace, "I would have seriously hurt someone without pine tar. I always had pine tar on my glove. It was so windy and dry, you

101

couldn't get any moisture on your hand—the ball would slip out, especially on the curveball. One time the ump came out and looked at my glove thinking he would find sandpaper. I had so much pine tar on my glove, you couldn't read the Wilson logo. He didn't say anything. I never got any [excess] on the ball. If you did that, you were an idiot."

Much was made of LaRussa giving Rogers a free pass. However, the rules say, umps don't need a manager's request to search a pitcher for illegal materials. The umpire can investigate at any time, and if he finds foul play, he must eject the pitcher, who is then slapped with an automatic ten-game suspension. (Before the 2007 season, the umpire had the option of issuing a warning.)

There is anecdotal evidence that umpires turn a blind eye (so to speak) to even blatant ball-doctoring. Jim Palmer tells of a pitching duel with famed spitballer Gaylord Perry, old Drool Hand Luke.

"When I came out to pitch the seventh inning," Palmer says, "his fingerprints were on the ball. You could see the smudge marks, some kind of foreign substance. If this was *CSI Baseball*, we would have had him. I tossed the ball to the umpire and said, 'Why don't we just take him to the precinct and book him?' The ump laughed."

On another occasion, Palmer was pitching against a notorious sandpaperer.

"He had scratched out all of [American League president] Lee MacPhail's autograph, which is a long name," Palmer says. "I threw the ball to the umpire and said, 'I think it may be illegal for me to use this.' He just laughed."

Maybe umpires just enjoy a good laugh.

KRUKOW TELLS OF A TIME LATE IN HIS CAREER WHEN HE HAD A SORE ARM AND, IN DESPERATION, HE TRIED A SCUFFBALL.

"A teammate showed me how to use sandpaper," Krukow says. "But I had the wrong grit. It was too rough and it scuffed the ball so much you could almost see the yarn under the cowhide cover. When I went out to pitch the first inning, I told myself I'd only use the sandpaper if I absolutely had to. The first batter tripled. So I scuffed the ball and struck out the side on eleven pitches. It was the most fun I ever had.

"Next inning I said to myself I wasn't going to use it again unless I was desperate. Andre Dawson hit one off the wall. So I scuffed the ball. The Cubbies' skipper was Stick Michael. He beefed about the ball, and Terry Tata kicked him out. Tata came out to me with four scuffed balls in his hand and said, 'I'm trying to work with you, don't [mess] around.' I said, 'Okay. But before you leave, can I have just one of those?'

Tata glared.

"I didn't get another out," says Krukow.

LORE—
Educational TV

HOW TO CHEAT IN SPORTS

In the major leagues, clubhouse televisions are for more than just watching *Deal or No Deal* with the sound off.

TV can be a great learning tool. At the start of every season, MLB sends a bulletin to each team to be posted in the clubhouse, stating that it is forbidden to use the TVs in the clubhouse, or the monitors in TV-camera wells next to dugouts, to watch the game in progress. The directive began in the '70s when some teams used spies in the stands or press box, with walkie-talkies, to steal opponents' signs and relay the info to the dugout, and then to hitters.

"I was a rookie with the [Milwaukee] Brewers in '83," says Tom Candiotti, who pitched sixteen big-league seasons for four teams. "Ted Simmons was our catcher, very intelligent. Every game, the first time we got a guy on second, Ted would run back to the clubhouse video room and get the other team's sign sequence from the monitor. It would take him only two or three pitches, and he'd know what they were using, their whole sequence.

"Next time we got a guy on second, we'd know the signs, and the runner would relay the info to the hitter. If it was going to be a breaking ball, he'd take a crossover lead. Fastball, he'd take a slide-step lead."

"WE WOULD MASSACRE THEIR PITCHER."

When Rex Hudler played in Japan, a teammate watching TV in the clubhouse would tell the hitting coach in the dugout, via cell phone, what pitch was coming.

"If it was a breaking ball, our hitting coach would yell, 'Ahhhh-ggghh!' It was so obvious what he was doing that it was hilarious, and it's flagrant cheating. But in Japan they're polite; they would never drill a batter [to retaliate for the cheat]. So what the other team would do, they'd all yell. Their whole dugout was going, 'Ahhhhggghh!' on every pitch."

There are other creative spying methods.

"When Frank Robinson was managing the [Cleveland] Indians," says former Indians infielder Duane Kuiper, "Robbie was convinced Bernie was stealing our signs, and Robbie was serious."

Bernie the Brewer was the Milwaukee Brewers' mascot, and his perch was a Bavarian chalet in the outfield.

HOW TO SELL A MISSED TAG OR TRAP

You just made a diving tag on a sliding runner. It was close, but you know you missed the tag, or maybe you're not sure. And if you're not sure, the ump probably isn't. With a little acting, you can remove all (or enough) doubt.

The Cheat

Do *not* lunge back and take another shot at the tag, hoping to catch the runner's foot off the bag. It's a low-percentage play, and it screams out your uncertainty that the tag was made. Instead, hold the ball in the air triumphantly.

In umpire school, umps are taught that when they're not 100 percent sure, they must "sell" their call with emphatic, decisive body (and verbal) language.

That's what *you* do: remove all doubt. And do it quickly.

Ron Washington, manager of the Texas Rangers and longtime third-base coach, says, "Never go back in. You have to sell it."

The same goes for trapping a sinking line drive, or going over the railing to "catch" a foul ball. Hold the ball high and give the ump the smug "catch face," then turn away, because it's such an easy call that you don't even need to see his hand signal.

HOW TO PEEK AT THE CATCHER

Once upon a time, the catcher would squat directly behind the plate, moving his glove to give the target. Baseball evolves. Now, as the pitcher begins his windup, the catcher shifts his entire body to set up behind his glove, to provide a better target and to be in a better position.

There is no written rule against the hitter peeking to see where the catcher has set up. There *is* an unwritten rule, and breaking it calls for retaliation.

"Sometimes the catcher's going to say something to the guy peeking, like, 'Knock it off,'" says Duane Kuiper. "Once you have a rep for peeking, they'll keep on eye on you from their bench."

Some catchers will signal the pitcher, "This guy is peeking; drill him." So it's risky, but high reward.

The batter isn't trying to steal signs. That would require a long, obvious gaze. The batter is looking for the catcher's setup location.

Three Ways to "Peek"

1 Wear dark wraparound sunglasses.

2 The sun or stadium lights might allow you to read the catcher's shadow.

3 Enlist a spy in the sky (or stands). Your coconspirator yells encouragement as the pitcher winds up. "Come on, Jimmy!" means inside setup; anything else he yells means outside. Add code words for high and low.

What good is this knowledge? Says former pitcher Tom Candiotti, "If you're a righty hitter facing a righty pitcher, if a pitch is coming inside, you pretty much know it's going to be a fastball, not a breaking ball or changeup. If it's away, it depends on the count. If it's 3-1 and the guy doesn't have good control of his off-speed pitches, you're probably looking for a fastball there."

HOW TO ALTER A BASEBALL'S MOLECULAR STRUCTURE

At the old ballpark, what plumps when it's cooked?

A hot dog?

Technically, yes, but the answer we're looking for here is "a baseball."

Thanks to the creative mind of a ballpark electrician, the world is rethinking the baseball. It's no longer the simple "rock" we came to know and love, but, rather, an organic object to be manipulated and adjusted to meet a team's needs.

The Colorado Rockies use humidification to keep their balls legal, but you can use the same science to make illegal balls. A little humidification or dehumidification will take baseballs out of spec and slant the game in your favor.

By MLB rules, the baseball must weigh between 5 and 5.25 ounces and measure between 9 and 9.25 inches in circumference. A ball exposed long enough to high humidity will plump up and exceed those specs, while a ball stored in low humidity will dry up and fall below the specs.

A heavy, humid ball favors pitchers. It weighs more and is spongier, so it doesn't fly as far, and because the cover is more moist and the seams slightly thicker, the ball is easier to grip. Conversely, a light, small ball benefits hitters.

Way before the Rockies found salvation by humidification, the Chicago White Sox used a similar tactic, though secretly. In the '60s and '70s the Sox were a scrappy, run-manufacturing team, and they had a secret advantage against power-hitting teams. The groundskeeper at old Comiskey Park was Gene Bossard. Gene's son, Roger, who succeeded his father as head groundskeeper, revealed in a newspaper interview, "In the bowels of the old stadium, my dad had an old room where the humidifier was constantly going. By leaving the balls in that room for ten to fourteen days, they became a quarter- to a half-ounce heavier."

If balls can be plumped up, why can't they also be dried out, like prunes made into raisins? They can!

So get out there and cook up the kind of baseball your team needs.

Materials

- 2 dozen baseballs
- postal scale accurate to one-tenth of an ounce
- (for plumping) 8 soup cans
- (for plumping) large (48-gallon or larger) plastic or metal picnic cooler
- (for plumping) 2 metal oven racks that will fit inside cooler
- (for shrinking) commercial food dehumidifier, which can also be used to dry beef, fruit, etc., for handy dugout snacks! Available online, starting at about $200. $\rightarrow$

Steps to Plump the Ball

1 Weigh 2 or 3 balls on the postal scale, tag or mark them, and keep a written record, with dates, so you can establish your own recipe, which will vary by climate and region.

2 Place 4 soup cans inside the cooler, one standing in each corner.

3 Place a metal rack on top of the soup cans.

4 Pour hot tap water into the cooler, to a depth of about 3 inches. Fill the rack with balls (see illustration on facing page).

5 Make another layer, using 4 more cans and another rack. Fill that rack with balls.

6 Close lid.

7 Replace the water once a day with hot tap water.

8 After a week, weigh the marked test balls to check progress. You're shooting for balls in the 5½- to 6-ounce neighborhood.

9 Once the balls have reached desired weight (they will also be larger), keep them in your steam box until you're ready to use them, or store them in another high-humidity container so they don't dry out. Keep the balls in storage until no more than two days before use.

Steps to Shrink the Ball

1 Weigh 2 or 3 balls on the postal scale, tag or mark them, and keep a written record, with dates, so you can establish your own recipe, which will vary by climate and region.

2 Place the balls in a dehumidifier on "beef jerky" setting.

3 Weigh your test balls every three days. Your goal is a weight of about 4 ½ to 4 ¾ ounces.

Alternative shrinking: Oven-bake the balls on low heat for several hours. However, it could take a few days or more to bake enough moisture out of the balls, and this could be costly, depending on your electricity rates.

(**Note:** Don't be confused by terminology! Traditionally, a lively baseball is said to be "juiced." However, a lively baseball is actually a ball that has had the juice sucked out of it.)

Sidebar: The Man Who Fixed Coors Field

The story of an honest man hardly belongs in a book on cheating, but give Tony Cowell his due: He changed the game, at least for one team.

Cowell is an electrician at Coors Field. For years he suffered along with other Colorado Rockies fans as Coors Field became synonymous with homerfests and ridiculously high scores. It was crushing to the spirit of Rockies pitchers, and to the morale of the team.

Everyone blamed Denver's thin, mile-high air.

Then one day Tony Cowell went elk hunting and his boots hurt his feet. He hadn't worn the boots all summer, and Denver's dry desert air had dried out and constricted the leather.

"I wondered if the same thing was happening to the baseballs," Cowell says. "If the leather cover of the ball shrinks up like my boots, it would squeeze the wool yarn winding more tightly and pull the laces tighter and lower, and the ball would be smaller and harder and would fly farther."

Indeed, pitchers likened Coors Field baseballs to cue balls—hard and slippery.

If it was thin air that was causing balls to jump out of Coors Field at a crazy rate, Cowell reasoned, there would be similar craziness in other sports. Denver Broncos quarterbacks would be able to fling a football thirty yards farther at home, right?

Maybe, Tony reasoned, it's not simply thinner air. He weighed Coors Field game balls—which are stored at the ballpark for weeks or months between delivery from the factory and game use—and found that most of them were well below MLB specs of between 5 and 5.25 ounces.

Denver's dry, high-desert air was sucking the moisture from the yarn and cowhide of the baseballs, rendering them lighter and smaller than the rules allow, with a slick, dry surface and lower seams.

"I did some crude testing," Cowell says. "I exposed balls to different levels of humidity and did drop tests. There was a difference. I did more research, and I learned that one property of wool is that it absorbs a tremendous amount of moisture. And when wool [the yarn wound around the ball's cork center] is moist, the ball bounces lower."

Using a large aluminum box made to store beer kegs, Tony built the Rockies a sophisticated, moisture-controlled ball-storage box that prevents moisture loss.

The new balls were put into play at the beginning of the 2002 season, without the knowledge of the players. Rockies hitters hit 97 homers at home that season, 30 homers under the average output of the first seven seasons at Coors Field. Opponents' homers in Coors Field didn't dip much that year, in part because the park's reputation prevented the Rockies from signing top pitchers, but the opponent-homer numbers have steadily declined since.

"The park started to play more like a normal park," Cowell says. "Now at least the Rockies have a fighting chance."

HOW TO DEKE THE RUNNER

On a well-executed hit-and-run, or on any ball hit through the right side, the runner on first steams around second and into third, unless the second baseman fields the ball—or the runner *thinks* the ball has been fielded.

The Cheat

1 You're the shortstop. There's no play at second base because the ball is through to the outfield, but you pantomime making a force play at the bag.

2 Assuming the runner isn't sure where the ball is, he, seeing the shortstop making the front end of a double play at second, must slide.

3 Result: no extra bag for the runner.

Keep in mind, this is a "save" tactic. Save it for a crucial game or game situation, so the runner isn't as likely to spot it as a ruse.

Cautionary Note: Another reason to use this deke sparingly is that you're causing a baserunner to make an unnecessary slide, so there's the slight injury-risk element. And runners don't like to be deked. As one former big-league infielder says, "Some guys consider this to be borderline chickenshit."

HOW TO USE SPIES TO DETECT THE PITCHER'S TIPS

Some pitchers tip their pitches—vary their mechanics slightly and unintentionally before and during their delivery, depending on what pitch they're throwing. Discovering a pitcher's tip is legal, unless you get help—as in spies.

The Cheat

Station a spy where he won't be noticed—in the stands, bullpen, somewhere beyond the outfield. He'll need binoculars, paper and pencil, and a signaling device. Have him chart/note any tendencies (i.e., pitcher always throws curveball on 2–1 count) and look for telltale "tips." Once he spots a tip, have a signal in place. For example, your spy in the bullpen or on the grass beyond center field is reading a newspaper. If he holds the paper up near his face, it's going to be a breaking ball.

In the major leagues, spying is sometimes done simply, and illegally, via clubhouse TV watching, taking advantage of the extreme close-ups and the center-field camera, since many "tips" can be spotted only from behind the pitcher—such as his grip as he holds the ball behind his back.

"When I played for Montreal, Graig Nettles was awesome," Rex Hudler says. "He'd sit in the clubhouse the first four innings, watching TV with a notepad. I was new to the team. I thought, 'These guys are *serious*.'

118

"John Franco was pitching against us. He had a circle change [a changeup requiring the ball to be tucked deep into the palm of the pitching hand]. We're in the pennant race; it's a tie game. [manager] Buck Rodgers sends me in to pinch-hit in the eighth or ninth, two guys on. Buck has a report from Nettles. He tells me, 'Nettles says Franco fans on a changeup, so spit on it.'"

Translation: *When Franco is gripping the ball to throw his change-up, he pushes his ball hand deeper into his glove, causing the fingers of his glove to fan out just a bit wider than usual. When he does that, don't swing, because he throws his changeup off the plate.*

"First pitch," Hudler says, "Franco fans his glove. Sure enough, it's a changeup, just outside. I watch it. Ball one. Second pitch, same thing, just outside, ball two. Third pitch, Franco narrows his glove. I know it's a fastball, and it's *mine*. I hit a three-run dinger."

LORE—
Tipping the Tippers

REX HUDLER PLAYED FOR THE PHILLIES IN '97. THE FINAL GAME OF THE SEASON WAS AGAINST THE FLORIDA MARLINS.

Hudler: "Florida had a lefty, Tony Saunders. Charles Johnson was their catcher. I was 9-for-10 off Saunders already that year, and that game I got hits my first two times up. My third time up, I dug in and I looked back at CJ and I said, 'I got him.' I shouldn't have said that, but I was feeling cocky. Whack, I got another hit.

"Now the game's over and I'm in the dugout, about to do the post-game radio interview. And here comes Charles Johnson, through *our* clubhouse, and you never see that. He looks worried, and he comes up to me and goes, 'Hud, *please* tell me what you got on Saunders.' They're going into the playoffs and if Saunders faces a hitter who knows what I know, Florida is dead. My first thought was, 'Don't tell him.' But I'm retiring, that was my last game, so I say, 'On his breaking ball, he wiggles the index finger that's sticking out of his glove.' CJ hugged me.

"I watched the playoffs on TV, Game 3 of the NLCS. Saunders is starting, and he's got a leather patch sewn over the exposed finger on the glove hand."

Saunders pitched a solid 5.1 innings, and Florida beat the Atlanta Braves.

HOW TO MANAGE
A SWAMP

The groundskeeper can be your secret weapon. He can:

- Slant the foul lines. Slant 'em toward the infield or away, depending on whether you have a good bunting team or are facing a good bunting team. "It's fairly easy to do and no one can tell," says a major league groundskeeper. "If you slant it away, there's no way a bunt along the line stays fair."

- Change the visitors' bullpen mound. Lower it, raise it, or change the slope. Force their pitchers to go through a period of adjustment to the real mound.

- Water the dirt in front of home plate and/or rake it up; or keep it dry and roll it hard. Sinkerball pitchers want a soft landing for balls chopped into the dirt. "If you water the dirt or rake it up, the ball just dies," our groundskeeper says. "Water works best. We have guys who throw splitters [sinking pitches]; I don't want that first hop chopping over the infield. I give it a little extra water in the morning, and just before the game."

- Water and/or rake the first-base leadoff area to slow down a running opponent.

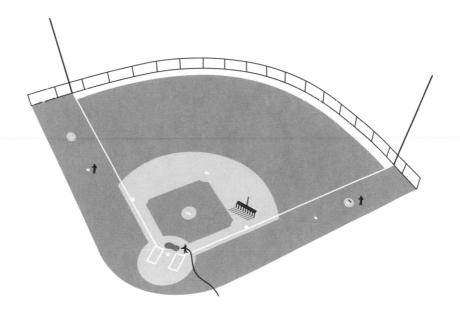

123 BASEBALL

LORE—
The Legend
of Matty Schwab

In August 1962, the Giants trailed the league-leading Dodgers by five and a half games when the Dodgers came to San Francisco's Candlestick Park for a three-game series.

THE DODGERS' MOST DANGEROUS OFFENSIVE WEAPON WAS SHORTSTOP MAURY WILLS, ON HIS WAY TO A RECORD-SHATTERING 102-STEAL SEASON.

Giants manager Alvin Dark instructed groundskeeper Matty Schwab to soak the first-base area during pregame field prep, turning Wills's launching pad into a swamp.

The Dodgers protested mightily, and before the third game the umpires ordered the groundskeepers to do something about the standing water. No problem! Schwab and his crew dumped several wheelbarrows of sand onto the field, providing Wills with basepaths made of quicksand.

The Giants swept the series, finished the regular season tied with the Dodgers, and won a three-game playoff to advance to the World Series.

OVERTIME—"Cheating is baseball's oldest profession," wrote Thomas Boswell, considered by many the poet laureate of baseball writers. "No other game is so rich in skulduggery, so suited to it or so proud of it."

—One reason baseball is cheater-friendly is that the payoff is so immediate and significant. If a pitcher loads up a ball by wetting it or nicking it, he can go from meatball-chucker to Hall of Famer. If a batter can, by theft, learn what the next pitch will be, and its location, his chance of success soars.

—Exhibit A: The Shot Heard 'Round the World, Bobby Thomson's home run that put the Giants into the 1951 World Series, was allegedly the product of a Giants spy in center field stealing the opposing catcher's signals and relaying them to the batter.

—Why are illegal pitches so effective? Because hitters hate breaking balls, and all cheat pitches are breaking balls. Says MLB veteran Rex Hudler, "Hitters—all of 'em—love heaters [fastballs]. No hitter ever says he loves breaking balls. It's always, 'I want that gas, I'm gonna turn that shit around [hit it out].'" Hitters just want to swing. As former reliever Stu Miller, king of the changeup, said, "Even if they have a PhD in physical education, most hitters are idiots once they get in the batter's box."

—Wise players make friends in low places. Game balls are usually rubbed with mud before a game to remove the factory shine and slickness. The umps do it, or they farm out the task to someone working in the home clubhouse. According to one source, Cy Young Award–winner Randy Johnson always has the ball-rubber rub the balls extra-dark, so the batter has a harder time seeing his pitches.

—Says Duane Kuiper, former second baseman for the Cleveland Indians "The legendary Bossard brothers [groundskeepers for the Chicago White Sox], they'd really go the extra mile for you. If I gave 'em a box of cigars every month, I could not find a pebble on my side of the field." Gene Bossard created Bossard's Swamp, a mudhole in front of home plate that bene-fited the White Sox sinkerball pitchers of the '60s.

—Two more tricks credited to Gene Bossard: Storing balls in a cold, humid room for two weeks until they soaked up a half-ounce of moisture, and secretly moving each of the bases one foot closer to home plate, reducing the distance from ninety feet between bases to eighty-nine, benefiting the team's speedy slap-hitters.

—No, pitchers and catchers don't necessarily have bad breath. When the parties cover their mouths with their gloves at a meeting on the mound, they do it to deter lip-reading opponents.

—You gotta be subtle. Hudler again: "When I was at Pawtucket [minors], we had a sign—if you lead off base with your right leg first, it's a breaking ball; left leg, fastball. I got on second, saw the sign for breaking ball, lifted my right leg like I was getting on a horse. Our guy got a hit. Next time I'm up, first pitch is at my head, next pitch is at my chin. The catcher said, 'If you steal our signs and relay 'em [again], we'll drill your ass.'"

—Tom Candiotti: "I used a corked bat for batting practice. A catcher with the Dodgers had one. There was a guy in Cleveland who corked; he did it for guys around the league. It made a big difference, it really did. There was a short area in left field at Dodger Stadium. I could hit the ball out of the park there, but with the corked bat I could hit it out even to deep left-center."

—George Frazier, who pitched in the big leagues in the '70s and '80s, always denied accusations that he applied a foreign substance to the ball. Domestic substance, sure.

—Gaylord Perry didn't get off scot-free. He was ejected from a game for throwing a doctored ball— in the twenty-first season of his twenty-two-year career. Perry feted his three-hundredth win by wearing a T-shirt reading: "300 wins is nothing to spit at."

— *Sports Illustrated* columnist Steve Rushin summed it up: "Cheating is to baseball as Bernoulli's principle is to fixed-wing aircraft—the invisible constant that keeps everything aloft."

0201

001

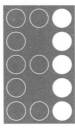

1
2
3
4
5

CH. 4

THERE IS NO UNIVERSAL SPORT, BUT THERE IS A UNIVERSAL IN SPORT: CHEATING.

And there's no point in searching for a common motivation for cheating. Cheating, in the final analysis, is its own reward.

As French poet Max Jacob said, "When you get to the point where you cheat for the sake of beauty, you're an artist."

Take auto racing. Please.

John Soares was once the crew chief for Dale Earnhardt's NASCAR team, and he's been involved in many other types of high-level auto racing. Asked his estimate of what percentage of racing teams at the top levels of the sport are cheating, or trying to, Soares says: "All of 'em."

You'd kind of expect that. NASCAR racing is simply a modern version of driving a car with courage and speed in order to cheat the government out of liquor taxes. Plus, the opportunities for mechanical cheating are endless in big-time racing. Sponsors pour huge amounts of money into NASCAR and other forms of auto racing, and they expect a return for their money. So the pressure to perform well and win, and therefore the temptation to cheat, is staggering.

Now Soares runs a little dirt track in the San Francisco Bay Area, a million miles from the pressures of big-time racing, where it's all about the fun and the pure spirit of neighborly competition. And yet everyone still cheats.

"The littlest classes are the biggest cheaters," Soares says. "We'll have a guy take a $400 carburetor out of the box and modify it with an illegal part that costs $1,400. For a trophy."

Lord, we love to cheat.

Some sports feature more cheating than others, but it's not a matter of honor or character—it's a function of opportunity. There are a zillion ways to illegally enhance a race car, but limited ways to cheat at Wimbledon's Centre Court, surrounded as it is by eagle-eyed umpires and judges and queens and princes. Other than by quick-serving, stalling, receiving illegal coaching, faking an injury to buy time . . .

135

NASCAR:
THEIR CHEATIN' HEARTS

There are 1,000,001 ways to cheat in auto racing, and that's before the driver ever crawls into the car.

NASCAR (Nextel Cup) racing was started by cheaters—moonshiners evading government agents. The first NASCAR race in 1949 was won by Glenn Dunaway, who was promptly DQ'd for illegal shocks. NASCAR has cracked down on cheating in recent years, but teams never stop trying.

The following cheats were all successful, though most are now obsolete owing to stricter enforcement. The list is courtesy of a very high-ranking NASCAR official, and John Soares, former crew chief for the late Dale Earnhardt and now manager of the Antioch Speedway in Antioch, California.

- Replace carburetor restrictor plate (no longer used) with alloy plates that evaporate when exposed to racing fuel.

- To beat the 3,800-pound-minimum rule, install secret cells in the car's frame and fill with 200 pounds of either buckshot or water, with holes at the bottom of the frame. The holes are covered with tape, which disintegrates in the heat of the race, dropping the load.

- Replace the legal fuel tank with a much larger tank, then seal the big tank with counterfeit NASCAR inspection tape. This cheat requires the driver to pretend to run out of gas at the finish line.

- Drill tiny holes in the wheels so tire air pressure bleeds down below legal minimum for better traction.

- To fool cylinder-volume test, shove a scented tissue into the cylinder to be tested (testers always test the same cylinder). The sticky chemical on the scented tissue hinders sealing and causes low (and legal) displacement reading.

- Bore the to-be-tested cylinder smaller than the other (illegal) cylinders.

- Soak the tires in chemical to soften the rubber. Says the NASCAR official: "I've seen garages with elaborate rotisserie systems for soaking tires in a shallow bath of fluid."

- Skew the body shape (now all but impossible with the Car of Tomorrow). Slant the roof to one side. Or distort the entire car in the shape of a banana by tweaking some front parts (bumper, etc.) to the right and some rear parts (roof and rear window) to the left, leaving center line of the body within template specs. "The banana shape was a huge aerodynamic advantage," the official says. Before templates, one team built an entire car to seven-eighths scale, undetectable to the eye. Smaller is faster.

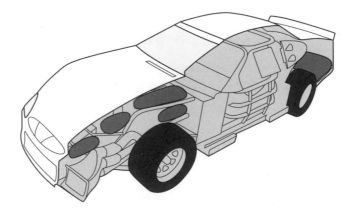

137

ICE HOCKEY: HOW TO SKATE AROUND THE RULES

Three EZ ice hockey cheats:

- Fighter sweaters. If you're paid to fight, the last thing you need is a jersey your opponent can use as a weapon against you, grabbing it to jerk you off-balance and constrain your punches.

  In the NHL, jerseys are required to have tie-downs to hook them to the pants, so the fighter can't slip out of the encumbering garment. Some players either tie the tie-down loosely or forget to tie it.

  Others wear extra-baggy sleeves, so if your foe grabs your sleeve you still have plenty of room to throw punches. The fighter might also have the seam of the sleeve sewn with light stitches, which bust when pulled.

- Goalie gear. At the NHL level there is much equipment regulation; at lower levels, not so much.

  Illegal modifications include extra-baggy pants to close up that five-hole; extra pads on the inside of legs, same reason; extra-loose jersey; oversize pads.

- Stick tricks. The rules regulate the amount of curve on the stick blade. Limits are pushed.

"I always had three sticks," says Jamie Baker, NHL star for ten seasons and now a radio color commentator for the San Jose Sharks. "One stick was for regular play; it was probably illegal. I had one stick I was sure was legal, for the end of the game. And one stick for penalty killing; it was too long. I didn't use it often, and its purpose was to poke-check.

"In the playoffs I used the stick with the legal curve all the time; I couldn't afford a penalty. I would also use a longer stick in practice when we were getting skated by the coaches, because I didn't have to bend over as far."

Rob Zettler, a fourteen-year former NHLer and now an assistant coach with the Sharks, says he would shave the heel of his stick, allowing the stick to pass a curve test even though it had an illegal curve.

SOCCER: HOW TO "HELP" THE REF

The U.S. national men's team has never been a force in international soccer, and this is partly due to a failure to communicate. In big-time men's soccer, flopping or diving is considered an essential tool for alerting the ref that you've been fouled.

Germans call the diver *schwalbe*, a low-flying swallow, but Americans insist on soaring like eagles. American men seem to consider the flop unmanly, but in fact it is very manly—the dive is relatively rare in women's soccer.

The Cheat

1 Your opponent has fouled you, or has come darn close to fouling you, and you must alert the referee. Simply fall down. The more inelegant the flop, the better.

2 Stay down. If you pop right back up, whether or not you get the call, you have exposed yourself as a phony and you might never get another call.

3 Writhe, grimace, cry in pain, and grab a body part (one of your own)—a leg is the most common.

4 In extreme cases, and if the game situation allows, milk your dive long enough for the stretcher crew to be brought onto the field. Allow the trainer to treat your injury with soccer's "magic sponge," with its miraculous healing powers. Stagger back to your feet. Or:

Take the stretcher ride off the field, hang out on the sideline for a few minutes, stagger courageously back into the game.

The soccer ref might be the most overworked official in sports. He can't see everything; he needs help.

FIFA has tried to crack down on diving by instructing refs to give yellow cards for obvious dives, but: "I never give a card for a dive," says one NCAA official. "It's just too hard to see everything; I can't assume the player is diving. And I never laugh at a diver, no matter how obvious it seems. I almost laughed at a guy once. It was such an obvious dive. Then I looked and he had a broken ankle; it was bent sideways, completely L-shaped."

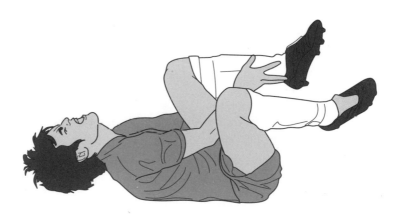

GOLF: HOW TO IMPROVE YOUR GAME WITHOUT IMPROVING YOUR GAME

Six EZ golf cheats, compliments of a top amateur golf official:

- With a tight lie in the fairway or a deep lie in the rough, firmly step down directly behind your ball, effectively lifting your ball to a better lie.

- When your ball comes to a rest near a tree or bush, "gather" the branches behind your back—stand on 'em—to clear the way for your backswing.

- When taking relief from an artificially surfaced cart path (immovable obstruction), drop on the most advantageous side of the path, even though you are required to go to the "nearest point of relief." Why drop behind a tree when you can give yourself a wide-open shot?

- Don't take that lost-ball stroke-and-distance penalty. The rules say you need "reasonable evidence" to conclude that your ball came to rest in a water hazard or lateral water hazard, but who's got time to call an attorney? Give yourself the benefit of the doubt.

- When you're entitled to one-club-length relief from abnormal ground conditions and immovable obstructions, use the imaginary stretch built into your longest club. What's a few inches? You're here to play the course, not survey it.

When marking and lifting your ball on the green, place your coin behind the ball before lifting, then replace the ball in front of the coin. You'll gain only about two inches, but do it for eighteen holes and you've gained three feet!

GOLF: HOW TO GET RELIEF

A golfer is entitled to relief—lift, clean, and drop no closer to the hole—if his or her ball rests in casual water, defined as "a temporary accumulation of water."

Ron Salsig, tour-player-turned-sportswriter, relates: "In the San Francisco City Championship in about '65, I was paired with a guy who wound up with a bad lie. He pissed on the ball and declared it casual water."

GOLF: HOW TO GET INTO YOUR OPPONENT'S HEAD

Two tips from a former touring pro who requested anonymity:

- "If it's head-to-head and the other guy is going good, either slow way down or speed way up. I found that slowing down usually works best, but it depends on the guy you're playing. Normally, the guy gets two up on you, he wants to keep moving right along, he's feeling good, he doesn't want to cool off. I'd take all the time in the world, and you could see the guy getting fidgety."

- "On the tee, you're playing with a guy who doesn't know the course. You don't say, 'That's where you want to go, over by that tree on the left.' Instead you say, 'You don't want to go right here, that's trouble.' You tell him where *not* to go. His brain doesn't hear 'don't.'"

Sidebar: Cheating the Golf Cheaters

Three true stories from members of The Golf Nut Society (Ron Garland, founder and Head Nut):

"In college, I was going to play my rival from another school, so the night before the match I had a guy I knew who went to that other school bang on my rival's dorm room door several times during the night. I paid the guy $15.

"I lost the match and later found out that my rival had stayed at his girlfriend's place that night."
—Ed Randolph

"Our fourth was Rick, who was rumored to be loose with the rules. On a par 5, Rick teed up last. I noted that he was hitting a new Titleist. He skied it toward the right OB line, out of sight.

"The rest of us found our shots and went to help Rick look for his. I found it in the first cut, a shiny new Titleist. I said, 'Hey, Rick, are you hitting a Maxfli red dot?' He said, 'Yeah, that's it!' I said, 'Too bad, this is a Titleist,' and I put it in my pocket. We never did find the Maxfli."
—Stephen Estopinal

"On dewy San Francisco mornings, observant Golf Nuts know to look at the line in the wet grass made by putts of previous groups. You get a free 'read.' My friend and competitor takes his putter handle and draws a false line from the hole to various ball positions, to throw off those who follow."
—Anon.

BOWLING: HOW TO ROLL WITH THE BEST

Six ways to improve your game:

- Drill your ball off-center. A ball that is top-heavy or side-heavy hooks harder and hits the pins harder—and is illegal. United States Bowling Congress rules allow a maximum weight difference of three ounces between the top half of the ball (the finger-hole side) and the bottom half. The left and right hemispheres must weigh within one ounce of each other.

  In the old days of solid-core balls, bowlers would buy a sixteen-pound ball and an eighteen-pound ball, saw each ball in half, then glue a heavy half to a light half. Scales were developed to detect these "dodo balls," and in USBC tournaments, balls are carefully weighed and checked for balance. Not so in smaller tournaments, leagues, and other matches. Find a ball driller willing to accommodate your needs. You could do it yourself, but an extensive knowledge of ball-core makeup is necessary.

- Load up your opponent's ball. Place a dab of Easy Slide (a slickening agent) or Pro Grip (a tacky agent) on the back of your bowling hand. Talcum powder or hand lotion will also work. Standing at the ball rack, dip a finger of your off-hand into the dab of goo and secretly wipe a bit of it on the inside rim of the thumb hole of your opponent's ball.

- Drill and fill. To make a ball illegally imbalanced, drill one or two holes two inches deeper and insert ball berrings, lead weights, or liquid mercury. Cover the fill with resin plug(s). After the ball passes weigh-in inspection, remove plugs(s) and fillers.

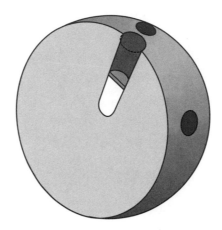

- Adjust your ball for the conditions. To make your ball bite better on slick lanes, sand one side with sandpaper or a scouring pad. This is illegal when done during a tournament or league play. To avoid detection, sew the scouring pad to your hand towel.

  If the lanes are too tacky and you need to straighten your ball, apply oil or STP to the ball's track line.

- Put the brakes on your opponent. Note your foe's foot-slide area near the foul line. "Burn rubber" by dragging the rubber heel of your bowling shoe hard on his spot, depositing a small amount of rubber to disrupt his foot slide.

  Or, drip sweat from your forehead onto his slide area.   →

- Plant seeds. "Bowling is a mind game," says John Ruckey of Lane 41 Pro Shop at Earl Anthony's Dublin Bowl in Dublin, California. He offers these tips:

In warm-ups or early in the match on a nonessential roll, slide your ball into the right gutter while trying to pick up the ten pin and make an audible comment like, "Gee, there's a lot of oil. My ball didn't move." Your opponent will compensate and miss his next ten-pin wide left.

Bowl in tennis shoes. This is legal unless the shoes have "soft rubber soles or heels that rub off on the approach." Says Ruckey, "I bowl in tennis shoes. They don't leave marks or rubber on the lanes, but my opponent doesn't know that. He's thinking, 'That guy is messing up the approach.'"

In warm-ups, lurch and pretend to stick near the foul line, then mutter angrily or make a comment about the sticky approach.

LACROSSE: HOW TO GEAR UP

Anything you can get away with in ice hockey pretty much goes in lacrosse, too. Johnny Meridian, general manager of the San Jose Stealth of the National Lacrosse League, offers these tips:

- Goaltenders' arm pads must meet caliper specs before the game, but when pads are tightly taped down to pass inspection, the tape tends to loosen or fall off between inspection and face-off, and the pads get wider.

HOW TO CHEAT IN SPORTS

- The lacrosse version of the flop. "A lot of helmets fly off indoors," Meridian says. "Some players keep 'em loose and flip 'em off when they get hit, to dramatize a penalty. The ref sees the helmet flying . . ."

- Baggy, saggy shorts for the goalie, to help plug that five-hole.

- A gusset sewn in the left arm of the goalkeeper's jersey. "They lift their arm and they look like a flying squirrel," Meridian says.

WATER POLO: HOW TO DRAW A FOUL

For a sport that is played in the water, water polo is kinda dirty. There are many tricks, but this one is easy and effective for escaping a situation where your defender is on you like a jellyfish.

The Cheat

1 You have the ball in your right hand, arm high, left shoulder aimed at man guarding you. You're closely guarded.

2 Form a hook with your left hand, palm facing out; reach out and set the hook around your opponent's waist and power-pull yourself around him. It's identical to the old basketball hook, where you hook your defender around his waist or upper legs and dribble past him while pushing him back and away—only, in polo, the dirty work is underwater, out of view.

3 Now you've got open water, and the defender must either let you swim deeper into his territory or commit an obvious foul by climbing over your back or grabbing one of your arms.

150

Bonus polo cheat: Goals normally sit on the water, supported by floats. On some goals, the side-rail floats wrap around the metal frame, like a fist around a broomstick, and slide in some fashion. When the action is at the opposite end of the pool, the goalie slides the side floats toward the rear of the cage, thus causing the top front rail of the goal to drop by two or three inches. Voila! Smaller goal.

HORSESHOES: HOW TO SKEW A SHOE

Three ways pitchers illegally improve the performance of the horseshoe, according to Casey Sluys, promotion and publicity director for the National Horseshoe Pitchers Association:

- With a file, sharpen the points of the shoe, for better penetration of the clay and increased chance of a ringer.

- Heat the shoe and widen the gap beyond the legal 3 5/8 inches.

- Weld the toe calk (the raised, cleatlike nub at the closed end of the shoe) higher, lower, or wider for better grip, less slide, etc.

For tips 2 and 3, you'll need to beg or borrow (not steal; we don't want to encourage bad habits) some heating/welding equipment, or find yourself a village smithy.

Note: "These [doctored] shoes are normally confiscated during an NHPA-sanctioned tournament," says Sluys.

Sluys says some pitchers use the pregame handshake as an opportunity to gain an edge.

"They'll squeeze your hand hard to make it sore and get you to thinking about their attempt to injure you. We had one guy who would grip so tight he would bite his tongue. After about two of his handshakes I refused any more."

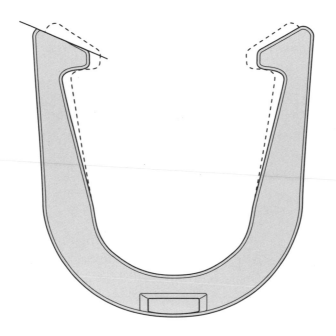

KICKBALL:
HOW TO GET A LEG UP

Four common kickball cheats, from Tiffany Ficklin, director of events and PR for the World Adult Kickball Association, which has two thousand teams in twenty-five states:

- Ringers. Official rules prohibit changes in a team's original roster once the season begins. Some teams will use a non-roster player(s) in order to avoid a forfeit or to add oomph to the lineup.

- Kicking out of order. Rules prohibit a change in the kicking order once lineup cards have been exchanged before the game. "Mistakes" are sometimes made. The referee (a player from another team) does not keep track of the kicking order; it is up to the opposing team to spot an illegal kicking-order change, and that team must call the infraction while the kicker is up. (Penalty: Batter is out; second offense: forfeit.)

- Sticky gloves. The official rules are undergoing revision to address specific equipment issues, but at present there is a vague rule against use of outside implements and aids. Most sporting goods stores carry sticky-tacky football wide-receiver gloves and spray-on Stickum, either of which will improve your flycatching. Be sure to remove the gloves or wash your hands (carry a Wet-Nap packet) before postgame handshakes with the other team.

■ Fudging toward the plate. By rule, until the ball is kicked, no fielder (including the pitcher) may cross the invisible line bisecting the diamond from first base and third base. There is a lot of bunting in adult kickball, so an illegal rolling start toward the plate is useful.

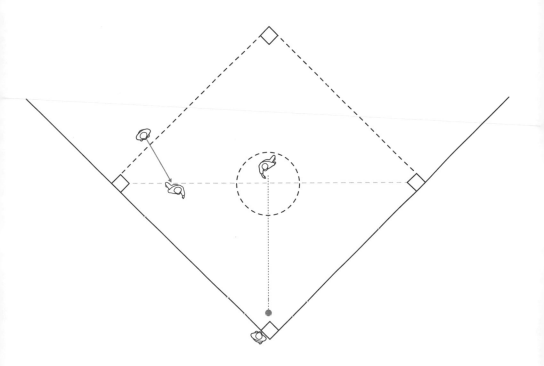

OVERTIME—In boxing, you've got the obvious cheats: head-butting, eye-gouging, biting, hitting below the belt, loading your gloves with horseshoes, or simply handing the judges cash bribes. To be creative in boxing, you have to cheat outside the box. In 1883, Charles "Kid" McCoy was fighting a deaf-mute. With a few seconds remaining in the fourth round, McCoy dropped his gloves and headed back to his corner. His opponent assumed the round was over, dropped his hands and turned away, and was quickly blindside KO'd by McCoy. Later in his life, McCoy did eight years in San Quentin for manslaughter.

—Basketball and soccer floppers are often accused of being unmanly, but faking falls is a very manly trait. Women seem to lack men's zest and aptitude for cheating in sports like basketball and soccer; women in both sports do far less flopping or diving than men. As one former college soccer ref says, "Girls don't do that kind of shit. They play soccer."

—Speaking of soccer, the most famous cheating incident of all time might be the Hand of God goal scored by Argentine legend Diego Maradona, against

HOW TO CHEAT IN SPORTS

England in the quarterfinals of the 1986 World Cup. Maradona, while attempting a header against the taller English goalkeeper, struck the ball into the net with his left fist. The referee didn't see the foul and allowed the goal. Argentina went on to win 2–1, then won the World Cup. Maradona described the goal as "*Un poco con la cabeza de Maradona y otro poco con la mano de Dios*," or, "A little with the head of Maradona and the other little with the hand of God." Years later Maradona admitted he got away with murder.

—How do you cheat in yachting? In 1968, in London's *Sunday Times* Golden Globe around-the-world yacht race, Donald Crowhurst pulled a Rosie Ruiz, shortcutting the course and hiding out on land while sending phony radio reports indicating he was in second place. Nigel Tetley, trying desperately to overhaul Crowhurst for second-place money, capsized and was knocked out of the race. When Crowhurst got the news, he showed his sporting side, jumping off his boat and committing suicide by drowning.

—Who was Rosie Ruiz? Rosie won the women's division of the 1980 Boston Marathon in record time, but it was quickly determined that she had run only the final mile of the race, conserving her energy by skipping the first 25 miles, 285 yards. The motivation for and details of her deception remain a mystery. Ruiz was stripped of her title, of course. Today she lives in South Florida and admits no wrongdoing in that race, but her legacy remains the gold standard for blatant cheating. Rosie kept her medal.

—It was a proud moment when the Spanish wheelchair basketball team won the gold medal at the 2000 Paralympic Games in Sydney. It was a less-proud moment when the team had to forfeit its gold. One team member blew the whistle and revealed that ten of the twelve players had no physical handicap (though they were clearly ethically challenged).

—Television is a good cheat spoiled. The intrusion of TV, with its close-ups and replays, has made cheating much more difficult in such sports as cricket (see page 89), baseball (see Kenny Rogers, page 101), and golf. Big Brother is always watching. But where there's a will . . .

—One fairly-famous PGA golfer has been rumored to pull out his three-wood when his ball is in the rough, tamp down the high grass or weeds behind the ball with the big clubhead to clear a swing path, then put the wood back in his bag and pull out an iron.

—The most common cheat in golf: sandbagging, or illegally inflating one's handicap.

—A dream match in golf would be former president Bill Clinton, who invented the presidential mulligan, versus North Korean leader Kim Jong-Il, who, according to official Korean news sources, aced eleven of eighteen holes the first time he played golf.

—An unknown golfer once said, "It's not that I really cheat at golf. I play for my health, and a low score makes me feel better."

ACKNOWLEDGMENTS

I couldn't have done it without:

- My wife, Kathleen, on whom I would never cheat. She kept my competitive edge sharp while this book was being assembled.

- The Chronicle Books team: editor Kevin Toyama, he of the serious creative chops, mad patience, and relentlessly upbeat outlook; copy editor David Sweet; designers River Jukes-Hudson and Brett MacFadden; illustrator Arthur Mount; production associate Yolanda Accinelli; and associate managing editor Doug Ogan and managing editorial assistant Evan Hulka.

- All the cheaters, and observers of cheaters, who shared their insights and stories with me, even though there was nothing in it for them except a free copy of this book. They have my sincere gratitude and appreciation. And as they're reading this, they also have the knowledge that whenever I promised a free copy of this book, I had my fingers crossed behind my back.